THE TRANSPORT CRISIS IN BRITAIN

SOCIALIST RENEWAL

The Transport Crisis in Britain

Philip S. Bagwell

Spokesman
for
European Labour Forum

First published in Great Britain in 1996 by
Spokesman
Bertrand Russell House
Gamble Street
Nottingham, England
Tel. 0115 9708318
Fax. 0115 9420433

Publications list/subscription details available on request

British Library Cataloguing in Publication Data available on request from the British Library.

ISBN 0-85124-597-8 cloth
ISBN 0-85124-598-6 paper

Printed by the Russell Press Ltd, Nottingham
(Tel. 0115 9784505)

Contents

vi

Acknowledgements

I am particularly grateful to Lilly Massicott whose help was invaluable in preparing this work for the press. I am greatly indebted to Matthew Waddup for the preparation of the graphics, and to his colleague Nick Cole for information on railway workers' pensions. John Armstrong gave unstintingly of his unrivalled knowledge of the British coastal trade. Marc Nussbaumer kept me fully briefed on French Government railway policy and Alan Sturt updated my understanding of the transport situation in the Netherlands. John Olney revealed anomalies of railway operations in the UK since privatisation. I enjoyed weekly lunchtime discussions with Lawrie Harries who, despite the many calls on his time, kept me well informed about recent developments in railway privatisation and trade union organisation. I wish to thank Theo Barker and Chris Wrigley for guidance about publishing. Jennifer Lawley was a most helpful correspondent on the transport situation in Wales. Discussions with Ken Hester put me wise on railway track matters. Alison Gowman kept me up to date on the London City Council's enlightened policy on cycle routes. Keen walkers David Rubinstein and Ann Holt were my source of information on the Pedestrian Association. I am grateful for the encouragement given me by Tony Simpson and Ken Fleet at Spokesman Books. Above all I am indebted to my wife, Rosemary, who encouraged me to continue writing despite the avalanche of papers and books in the front room of our house.

Preface

Individuals sometimes admit error. They may say, 'I was wrong, but I have learned the lesson of my mistakes. I will change my ways'. With governments and politicians it is generally different. They may see that they have blundered but do not like to admit it openly. They quietly change direction and hope that the general public will not notice it.

I have been a teacher of history all my working life. I have seen it as my task to encourage students to sift evidence on the causation of changes and to evaluate the economic, social, political and moral consequences of the past events they have been studying.

I believe that although events never repeat themselves exactly, we can learn to avoid the mistakes of the past. Increasingly in recent years my research has been into transport history and policy. In my journeys to and from the record offices and libraries of London and other metropolitan areas, in travels throughout the UK and attending conferences or going on holidays abroad, I have learned to appreciate the dedication of transport workers. I have noted the different policies adopted in other countries for the provision of passenger and freight transport. I have studied the policies of British governments in the light of these experiences.

This book is divided into three parts. The first part attempts a 'bird's eye view' or 'state we are in' description of the transport situation in the UK at the present time. The second is a historical explanation of how this state of affairs came about. In the third part alternative policies are advocated.

The Transport Crisis in Britain is not a comprehensive account of all that has happened in the history of the railways, motor car, heavy goods vehicles, inland waterways, coastal shipping and air traffic. Its purpose is to pinpoint the outstanding problems of the present day, explain their origins and advocate remedial action.

Philip S. Bagwell
London, July 1996

Figures

Tables

Chapter One
Forms of Transport and their Potential

Apart from a very few crofter communities dependent on the land they cultivate and the animals they raise for their subsistence, everyone in the UK relies on some means or other of transport. Manufacturing industry often draws its raw materials from far distant sources of supply. Factory workers, shopworkers, miners and those employed in the professions, distribution or personal services need to travel to their work-places. Although families and friends can exchange greetings by phone or the post, follow up contact is made by car, bus, coach, railway or air travel. Not all churchgoers live just around the corner from their place of worship. The groceries or domestic hardware purchased by the shopper have been brought to the store or supermarket often from distant sources of supply. Without good transport, businesses and family and community activity are impaired or rendered impossible.

The principal means of transport are walking, cycling, rail-ways, motor cycles, cars, motor vans, buses, airplanes, inland waterways, and coastal shipping. Each of these has its own advantages and limitations. The relative advantage of each compared with its rivals changes over time through the influence of technological innovation, the impact of wars, and government policies and the impact on them of the activities of pressure groups.

The great advantage of inland waterways is where delivery speed is not important but large loads have to be carried, they are very cost effective, since little energy is used in what is almost a frictionless system compared with road or rail. On the other hand canals provide a less flexible and secure service than do railways (where there are adequate branch lines) or motor vehicles.

Coastal vessels also have a competitive edge when it comes to the movement of bulky goods over long distances. The coaster's main costs are incurred at the beginning and end of each voyage, so that shorter trips are less economical, measured in pence or pounds per tonne kilometre, than are the longer ones.

With the spread of railways after the opening of the Stockton and Darlington line in 1825, steam powered trains enjoyed a virtual monopoly of long and medium to short distance transport for about a hundred years, though horse-drawn rulleys dominated railhead distribution until well into the inter-war years.

The railways dominance was due to their superior speed and their ability to carry a greater number of passengers than did horse-drawn coaches. Their vulnerability lay in their lack of flexibility when compared with motor vehicles and their backward technology in freight movements, manifested in their employment of small capacity wagons and the paucity of continuous brake fitments.

The bicycle was the subject of rapid technological change in the 1890s and early years of the twentieth century. Flora Thompson, in her classic Lark Rise to Candleford, noted the strangeness and short life of the Ordinary 'penny farthing' version compared with its successor the Safety which did not require the same degree of athleticism to master. At least until the end of World War II the bicycle was very popular with the working classes and those who were members of the Youth Hostels Association. In 1931, when there were only one million private cars on British roads, there were an estimated ten million cyclists.[1] The attraction of the bicycle was its relative cheapness. Postmen, dockers, railway signalmen on early shifts, policemen, nurses, and many others found this means of transport indispensable to get to work or enjoy rides on the still largely car-free roads. After 1945 there were further technical improvements, with alloys largely replacing steel, improved brakes, multiple gearing and lighter tyres made possible by the improved state of the roads. However the allure of the Austin Seven and the Morris Minor brought about the decline of cycling amongst those families enjoying a higher standard of living.

The great advantage of motor vehicles is their flexibility compared with water transport and the railways, making possible 'seamless web', door to door, journeys without the inconvenience of interchange at start and end of each trip. The disadvantage of motor transport are social and environmental when the capacity of the roads to accommodate vehicles reaches saturation point, bringing the economic waste of congestion, visual intrusion and air pollution.

There is a strong case for considering transport as a whole rather than looking at each means in isolation from the others. Canals have declined in importance not entirely because of their inherent weaknesses but because of the acquisitiveness and dominance of the railways in the 19th and early 20th centuries. The changed environment of the roads has played a large part in the reduction of walking as a means of gaining access to schools and shops. It does not make sense to study trends in railway passenger travel without reference to the twenty-fold increase in the number of private cars on the roads between 1931 and 1991.

There has never been a 'level playing field' in competition between different forms of transport. It has not been present in the area of long distance freight movement since, for journeys over about 120 miles, 38 ton road vehicles gain more benefits from the roads they use than the taxes (licence duty and petrol tax) they pay, while rail freight has had to pay a fair sum for the track it uses.

Government action or inaction can prevent a particular form of transport being used as fully as economic and social considerations would warrant. The Royal Commission on Canals of 1906-9 described as 'the most comprehensive study of the waterway system of the British Isles that has ever been made',[2] in its twelve volume report, advocated the widening of the canals to enable them to take 100 ton barges on what became known as the Cross. These were the links between Birmingham and Leicester to London; from Leicester, Barton and Nottingham to the Humber; from Wolverhampton and Birmingham to the Mersey and from Wolverhampton and Birmingham to the Severn. It considered the adoption of this plan would greatly reduce the price of coal and other raw materials. For example the cost of carrying coal from Leicestershire to London would be reduced from 6s 8d to 3s 10d a ton.[3] However the influence of the Railway Companies Association in parliament was strong at the time and it had a good advocate in the author E.A. Pratt whose books British Canals, (1906) and Canals and Traders, (1910) presented a well argued case against the Commission's proposals especially the recommendation that there should be state ownership of the key canal routes through a National Waterways Boards. Other business, including the introduction of national insurance, a Trade Disputes Act and

4

controversy over home rule for Ireland occupied the Asquith government's time until the outbreak of World War I when the creation of the Railway Executive Committee (REC) strengthened the influence of the Railway Companies Association and pushed plans for better canal utilisation into the background. Had the Royal Commission's recommendations been put into effect and had the Cross been maintained, canal transport would have had a better chance of realising it's innate potential in the inter-war years. The absence of a 'level playing field' between railways and canals was again demonstrated between 1914 and 1917 when the third of the canal mileage which was owned by the railways were under the control of the REC but the remaining two thirds were left to their own devices and were at a revenue-earning disadvantage compared with the Railway owned waterways which gained the lion's share of War Department orders. There was no possibility in 1919 of 'starting from scratch', with the canals gaining what they would have regarded as their rightful share of freight traffic.

In the UK the direction of transport policy has been determined to an unhealthy extent by the influence of specialist interest groups. Until about 1930 the Railway Companies Association exercised an undue weight on legislative policy and administration through, first, the Board of Trade and, after 1921, for a short time the Ministry of Transport.[4]

After 1932 when the British Road Federation was established to bring together a diversity of road transport organisations, the road lobby became increasingly dominant and was particularly manifest during the time that Ernest Marples was Secretary of State for Transport in the early 1960's.[5] A landmark in the prolonged attempt to curb the influence of the road lobby was the formation of Transport 2000, partly through the initiative of Sidney Weighell of the NUR, in 1971.[6] A quarter century after its formulation its influence has increased to the extent that Tory Secretaries of State have had to pay at least lip service to its contention, expounded in its bimonthly journal Transport Retort, that more and more motorway building is no answer to Britain's transport problem.

In contrast the tradition in France has been that there is a need for strong central government direction of transport policy. As an example of this in the 1990's there was a decision of the Council of

Ministers to approve on 14 May 1991 a Master Plan for high speed railways. Such a master plan was required by the terms of the basic French Transportation Law (La Loi d'Orientation des Transports Interieurs of 30 December 1982). Through this decision the first TGV route between Paris and Lyon was opened in 1984. This was no harebrained extravaganza. Mitchell P. Strohl wrote that 'it arose out of the traffic situation of the Paris–Lyon rail artery'.[7] He claims that local, provincial and regional opposition to the scheme could not have been overcome without the authority of the Law of 1982 and the French Council of Ministers. The Netherlands government's second National Transport Plan covering the period from 1990-2010 is a truly integrated plan covering all forms of transport, but the largest part of the investment programme (38%) is dedicated to the Dutch Railways (NS). When the Rail 21 plan was adopted by the Ministry of Transport and NS it was expected that the number of passenger-kilometres per year would double from 9 billion to 18 billion by 2010. In the summer of 1991 this was amended to 20 billion![8]

The above are some of the considerations which need to be borne in mind when examining the state of British transport in 1996, which is the purpose of Part I (chapters One to Five) of this book.

Chapter One: Notes

1. R. Watson and M. Gray, The Penguin Book of the Bicycle, (1978), p.143.
2. C. Hadfield, British Canals, (1950), p.229.
3. Ibid., p.232.
4. See G. Alderman, The Railway Interest, (1973) passim.
5. M. Hamer, Wheels within Wheels, (1987), pp. 18, 50, 54, 57, 64, 100 and 135, and W. Plowden,
   The Motor Car and Politics, 1896-1970, (1971), p.350.
6. S. Weighell, On the Rails, (1983), pp.24-25.
7. M.P.R. Strohl, Europe's High Speed Trains, (1994), p.104.
8. A. Sturt, 'Netherlands: Taking the Integrated Route', Transport, (May-June 1991), pp.73-75; see also the same author's 'Going Dutch', Town and Country Planning, (February 1992), pp.48-51; and Netherlands' Railways, News Release, (18 July 1991).

Chapter Two
Railways

According to the Major government's White Paper, New Opportunities for the Railways, published in July 1992, 'the efficiency of British Rail compared well with that of other European railways'. It was also claimed that 'the productivity of the BR workforce is among the highest of any European railway'. These claims were endorsed by British Rail whose Annual Report and Accounts revealed that in the year to 31 March 1994 the track kilometres run (loaded and empty) per member of staff employed were 3,463, compared with an average of 2,220 of the thirteen other member states of the Community of European Railways (CER).

But are these figures a true measure of the success of railways in Britain? If there is only one railway worker to every 3,463 of train kilometres run, is this a sign of success, or an indication of an inadequate service? If more and more stations are unstaffed, ticket machines are substituted for booking clerks and no member of staff is on hand at platforms to inform and reassure lonely passengers, is this an encouragement to travel by train or a reason for opting to travel by bus or car, or not to travel at all? It may be questioned whether railways are under, rather than over-staffed.

One measure of the attitude of governments to railways, and, by deduction, the attitude of the people that elect them, is the proportion of the Gross Domestic Product (GDP) allocated to their support. Figure 1 shows that throughout the last decade support for railways, from public funds, was well below that of the other European countries and in 1993-4, the last year before British Railways' privatisation, it was 0.18 per cent, compared with the average of other CER railways of 0.59 per cent. In other words, the European countries spent, on average, more than three times as much of their national income on railways as did the UK.

FIG.1 Support for railways from public funds as a proportion of Gross Domestic Product GDP.

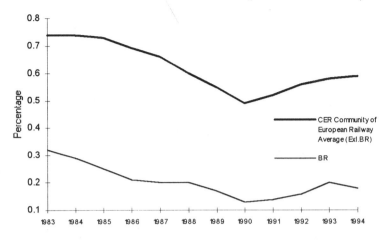

Source: British Railways Board: <u>Annual Reports and Accounts,</u> section International Performance Indicators.

Another indication of the degree of importance national governments have for their railways is the level of government grants as a proportion of total railway revenues. <u>Figure 2</u> shows that in the 1980's British Railways had the lowest proportion of total revenue derived from government grants of any of the European railways. At the start of the decade of the nineties it appeared that there was a more generous attitude by the British government. For the year 1990-91 payments by central government for railway operations rose by 20 per cent to £601 millions. However, this was only the second increase since 1983 and sums allocated were still more than forty per cent lower in real terms than the grant paid in 1983.[1] It was also the case that in 1990-1, in subsidy per head of population, BR spent only one fifth of the level of expenditure in France and Germany. In that year government grants formed only 17 per cent of BR's total revenue.[2]

8

FIG. 2 Grants from Central and Local Government
as a proportion of total railway revenues

Key:

BR	British Railways	NSB	Norwegian State Railways
DB	German Federal Railways	RENFE	Spanish National Railways
DSB	Danish State Railways	SJ	Swedish State Railways
FS	Italian State Railways	SNCB	Belgian National Railway Company
NS	Netherlands Railways	SNCF	French National Railway Company

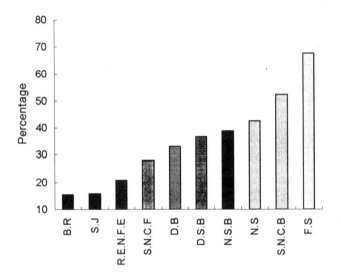

Source: International Union of Railways: <u>Statistics of
Individual Railways</u>, (1988) Table 72 p.94.

One of the important consequences of BR having lower
grants than did the railways of the CER was that it was obliged
to raise a larger proportion of its revenues in passenger fares
and freight charges than did its counterparts in Europe.
Throughout the period of the Thatcher and Major governments a
consistent policy was followed allowing passenger fares to rise
more steeply than the rate of inflation. This is illustrated in
<u>Table 1</u>.

TABLE 1 Real Rail Fare Increases Per Year Since 1980

Average increase per year after allowing for inflation

	(%)
1980-1985	+ 2.7
1986	+ 4.6
1987	+ 0.7
1988	+ 1.5
1989	+ 1.1
1990	− 1.1
1991	+ 4.6

Source: Hansard, Commons, 10 March 1992.

Between January 1987 and January 1993 when the Retail Price Index rose by 37.9 per cent, rail fares increased by 61.6 per cent. Major General Lennox, Chairman of the rail 'watchdog', the Central Rail Users Consultative Committee, stated that standard rail fares in the UK were roughly double those of other EC members. On 11 January 1993, in the House of Commons, Mr. Hardy asked the Transport Secretary if he 'would take the necessary steps to ensure that the fares charged for travel on BR are broadly in line with those which apply in other EC member states'. Mr. Freeman, speaking for John MacGregor, the Transport Secretary, declared that

fares could be reduced only if subsidies were increased. It would be wrong to ask taxpayers to fund bigger subsidies. Passengers who are the main beneficiaries of the service should bear as much as possible of the cost.[3]

Mr. Freeman did not apply to all transport modes the principle of all transport users paying the full cost of the particular form of transport they used. Motorists took for granted the 'free' use of the roads over which they travelled. They were subsidised in so far as they did not pay the costs of congestion, accidents and pollution. Road construction and maintenance were paid for out of taxation, local and national, and the revenue from car and van licences and fuel taxes did not meet all these costs.

High rail fares resulted in relatively low rail usage. A combined University of Leeds/BRB comparative study of European Rail Performance in 1979 commented that

It is important to note that the relatively low level of rail passenger traffic on BR is associated with the highest mean real fares on any railway considered (in purchasing power terms).[4]

In this survey the railways of Germany (West), Italy, France, the Netherlands, Norway, Sweden, Belgium, and Finland were compared.

In Britain the continuing low level of government subsidy and consequent high fares caused a steady reduction in the proportion of total passenger travel being made on the railways. It fell from 10 per cent in 1965 to 5 per cent in 1994, though BR's effort to retain the custom of groups of the population, such as students and senior citizens, were of value in maintaining a continuing high level of rail usage. Nevertheless, passengers compared the immediate, rather than the longer term costs, of the form of transport they used. A day return fare from London (Victoria) to Brighton was £11.90 in 1995 (£7.85 on a senior citizen railcard). The immediate cost of two people travelling to the same destination and back by car was no more than £10, with the added convenience of door to door travel.

One consequence of the high level of passenger fares on BR was that roads in Great Britain were the most congested in Europe. More passenger and goods vehicle miles were travelled on the roads of the Federal Republic of Germany, but the German road network was nearly one third larger than the British, so that the average number of vehicles per kilometre on British roads was higher.

As a result of BR having inadequate revenue support from Government, rail freight charges needed to be kept at a high level. Following the Beeching and later cuts there were also fewer rail depots for collecting goods for dispatch by train or for delivery by road. More freight was then sent all the way direct by road. Freight moved by rail fell from 142 million tonnes in 1982 to 103 million tonnes in 1993.[5]

The situation in the early 'nineties was that British freight trains were carrying smaller average consignments than were their counterparts on the European continent. Freight train loading (freight ton kilometres divided by loaded and empty freight train kilometres) was 267 tonnes, compared with 319 on CER.[6] The emphasis on quicker delivery times, to match or exceed the performance of road hauliers, meant that the economies of scale which were more possible on freight trains than in road haulage, could not be enjoyed. It was a wasteful situation. British Rail's freight trains were working at less than optimum capacity and at less than optimum frequency. At the same time British roads were becoming ever more congested as heavier vans obstructed the highway.

Although the British governments paid infrastructure grants for some projects between 1968 and 1974, grants towards railway investments were not generally given thereafter. BR was obliged to meet the costs of maintenance and any new replacement or development costs out of its own revenues.[7] Although the Leeds University/BRB survey found the British performance 'very good' it also reported that the level of investment per train kilometre was lower than on any of the other railways it studied. The most notable non-involvement of the British government was its refusal to make any grant for the construction of the Channel Tunnel, with the result that this project was financed (expensively) by 225 banks and with the further result that by the summer of 1995 Eurotunnel had a debt of eight billion pounds.[8]

In a ceremony in December 1979, introducing the University of Leeds/BRB study of comparative railway performance, Sir Peter Parker, Chairman of British Rail, said:

> On the basis of these comparisons we can now see that BR's relatively high fares are due neither to excessive wage levels, nor to poor productivity, but to relatively low support from the taxpayer for railways in Britain. We do not want to moan about that, but we do ask that it be noted. For instance, we have for some time suggested that BR's investment levels are inadequate.

Now these comparisons show them to be the lowest in Europe.[9]

Sir Peter's warnings were not heeded by the Thatcher governments of the 1980s. Through reductions in the Public Service Obligation grants and through the stranglehold of the External Financing Limit, the amount of taxpayers' money allocated to the railways was reduced. Half way through the next decade, Major General Lennox Napier, in his last Report as Chairman of the Central Rail Users' Consultative Committee, on 27 July 1995, returned to the theme of inadequate railway investment. He stressed that

There is a crying need for new and additional rolling stock and yet we see the decline of a viable manufacturing industry through lack of orders. In some areas, the service has become dependent on inadequate resources rather than on what passengers actually require. There is no spare rolling stock, and short formations of trains tend to occur more frequently as stock is withdrawn from service due to breakdown or overhaul. Older stock has been withdrawn from service without replacement, so there are over 2000 fewer coaches available now than there were six years ago.[10]

The Commons Transport Committee was given more precise figures of the decline in railway investment. The total (excluding the Channel Tunnel) fell from £1,013 million in 1990-91 to £665 million in 1993-94, the last year before privatisation.[11] The Committee pointed out that when Railtrack – the company made responsible from 1 April 1994 for the infrastructure, including the track, signalling and stations under the Railways Act, 1993 – took over, it

inherited a total of some 23,000 track miles of railway which have been starved of sustained investment for many years. The result is that the control and safety of the network is managed by a bewildering variety of equipment dating in some cases from the last century.[12]

The Institute of Railway Signal Engineers in its evidence noted that the age and safety of electrical signalling introduced in the 1950s and 1960s was causing concern. Lack of finance would appear to have delayed both renewal and improvement to these safety systems and the current indications are that this situation will worsen.[13]

In the all-important subject of investment in new rails the Transport Committee was given alarming information from the only UK manufacturer of rails, British Steel Track Products, which stated that

> in the period 1980 to 1985, BR replaced on average 2.1 per cent of its running rails each year. In the period 1985 to 1990 this had dropped to 1.3 per cent and in the latest period from 1990 to 1995, the figure has fallen further to an average of 1.1 per cent. Whilst some of this reduction is due to improved quality of rail, better track layouts and improved rolling stock suspension, a rail replacement rate of 1.1 per cent would mean that rails had reached a predictable life of over 90 years. Even British Steel admit that this is not possible.

A further cause for alarm about the British situation is that, by comparison, the national railways of both France and Sweden replaced an average of 2.7 per cent of their rails annually between 1991-1993 –more than double the BR replacement rate.[14] The situation with regard to rail fastenings (which secure the rails to the sleepers) was every bit as alarming. Pandrol Rail Fastenings Ltd reported that Britain 'was at the bottom of the European league' for the pace at which replacements were made.[15]

Uncertainty as to whether railway privatisation could be carried through successfully undoubtedly depressed orders for new and replacement rolling stock. The Railway Industries Association told the Transport Committee that there was a 'hiatus in orders' which brought a crisis to the stock manufacturing sector. Commuters on the East Kent line and other regions of the railway network bore witness to this fact in letters to British Rail and their local newspapers.

In the light of the above facts, the statement by the newly appointed chairman of the British Railways Board, John K. Welsby, in June 1995 that

> investment in the existing railway is not at a satis-factory level, and will not sustain the industry in the long run[16]

may come to be seen by railway enthusiasts as the understate-ment of the year.

The productivity of railway labour increased dramatically in the 1980s and early 1990s. The passenger miles travelled over this span of time fell slightly from 19,150 million in 1987 to 18,867 in 1994. The fall in freight traffic from 10,293 to 8553 net tonne miles in 1994 was more substantial but not so great as the fall in the number of railway employees handling the freight. In total the number of BR staff employed fell from 143,804 in 1987 to 115,446 in 1994, a decline of 28,358 or 15 per cent; real wages did not rise commensurately with this impressive rise in the productivity of the work force.

For the quarter century following the nationalisation of the railways in 1948 industrial relations in the industry were based very largely on consensus between management and the leadership of the three main trade unions, the NUR, ASLEF (the footplate workers union) and TSSA, the Transport Salaried Staffs' Association. Although there were often local disputes about the implementation of national agreements, there were only four national strikes between 1948 and 1981. Union leaders had more in common with the members of the BR Board when they were, to a greater extent, career railwaymen, than they did with boards after 1980 in which business leaders from outside industry or finance figured more prominently.

Many examples could be quoted of the way in which union leaders before 1981 cooperated with management in improving the efficiency of British Railways. When a crisis over railway pay developed in February 1951 the NUR agreed, as a condition of its members being granted a 7½ per cent rise, a package of 'Measures for Increased Efficiency'. The union's officers acknowledged 'the imperative need for the fullest cooperation with the Railway Executive in the elimination of waste of manpower in increasing efficiency and improving productivity within the railway industry'. This was no face-saving formula. A special Joint Committee of the Railway Executive and the railway unions was set up to promote these economies. In 1955 the volume of passenger and freight traffic was approximately the same as it had been in 1951, yet the number of railway workers fell by over 22,000 in the same period.

In 1967 railway management pressed for still further concessions from the unions on efficiency. Prolonged dis-cussions took place in Penzance and Windsor in 1967-8. BR was mainly concerned with the reduction in the number of separate grades of workers employed and their greater flexibility. The NUR's contribution to these discussions, published in a 21-page memorandum entitled Railway Wages, Structure, Pay and Productivity, was described by Len Neal, the leader of the management team, as 'an extremely imaginative and com-prehensive paper'. The new grade of 'Railman' was a product of the Penzance Agreement of July 1968. Men and women in this new grade could be called upon to carry out a great variety of duties, forty-one in number, from the loading and unloading of barrow traffic and the operation of mechanical sweepers, to the operation of carriage washing machines and the collection, folding and distribution of wagon sheets, ropes and packing. There was a parallel streamlining of the work of other grades in the railway service with the result that the number of railway employees fell by over 23,000 between 1968-70, though railway passenger traffic increased by more than a billion passenger miles, and freight traffic carried in 1970 was nearly a million ton miles more than it had been in 1968.[17]

Sometimes the railway unions took the initiative in promoting more modern practices. Noting that the pace of railway electrification was slower in Britain than it was in France and Germany, the NUR published a 16-page booklet in December 1978 called Railway Electrification in which the higher power-to-weight ratios, enhanced reliability, lower maintenance costs and environmental advantages of electric, as against diesel, traction were stressed.

With the election of a Tory government under Margaret Thatcher in May 1979 the direction of British railway policy was completely changed. The emphasis was more decisively switched to a policy of commercial viability in all aspects of railway operation. Superimposed on the business pressure to reduce costs, especially the costs of what was regarded as 'over-staffing', there was a particular antipathy to railway trade unions. After all, it was the Amalgamated Society of Railway Servants (ASRS), the precursor of the NUR, that had been the instigator at the Plymouth TUC in 1899 of the Labour Representation Committee, the predecessor of the Labour Party. So if rigorous cost cutting resulted in the reduction of the work force and the decimation of railway union membership, so much the better.

The big turning point in the relations between railway management and railway unions came with the Serpell Report Railway Finances, of 20 January 1983. At the beginning of the 1980s the BR Board considered that there was a lack of any sense of direction in the railway industry. In its Rail Policy statement of 25 March 1981 it asked the Secretary of State for Transport for a 'form of Contract for the Social Railway' which would give 'BR a clear sense of direction' for the future. The terms of reference which David Howell, the Transport Secretary, gave to Sir David Serpell and the three members of his team were

> To examine the finances of the railway and associated
> operations in the light of all relevant considerations,
> and to report on options for alternative policies and
> their related objectives, designed to secure improved
> financial results in an efficiently run railway in Great
> Britain over the next 20 years.

Sir Peter Parker, Chairman of British Rail, gave a warm welcome to the committee and approved the objectives which it had been given. The right-wingers on the Tory government back-benches and Margaret Thatcher's closest advisers were dissatisfied with the broad character of the committee's terms of reference. Their primary aim was to end state involvement and support for the railway. Therefore, in September 1982, some months after the committee had begun its hearings, David

Howell wrote to Sir David Serpell, directing him to give priority to cutting railway operational costs over the next five years. This set the seal on railway policy in the years before privatisation in 1994. Every other consideration was to be subservient to that of commercial profitability.

What happened to the Bedford–St Pancras services in 1983 illustrated the new emphases of policy. BR demanded driver-only operation of trains, on the grounds that new communication technologies had made the provision of a guard an unnecessary extravagance. The NUR contended that the guard should be retained to protect the train and the passengers from vandalism and assault and to collect revenue from fare-dodgers. The dispute was taken to the Railway Staffs National Tribunal, an important part of the established negotiating machinery. This body recommended a six months' trial of the NUR proposals. Halfway through the trial period the London Standard (8.3.84) reported that the scheme was 'a runaway success', saving BR £7,000 a week. This revelation did not please the Thatcher cabinet which arranged for the abolition of the Tribunal.

The brunt of the cost cutting so vigorously pursued by governments in the 1980s and 1990s was borne by the railway worker. In a table of Minimum Rates of Pay in Comparable Industries, published in January 1988, railway staff had sunk from fifth place in 1975 to ninth place in 1987.[18] However, the rewards of those who worked on the railway declined in relative terms, even further by the 1990s. In September 1992 the Labour Research Department published a 'League Table' of lowest basic manual pay. It reported on 387 separate pay agreements. BR's manual worker grades came 385th. Although the BR Board declared that there was 'no general problem of low pay' in the industry, in that month 33,260 of its 78,138 weekly paid workers were receiving below £154.72 a week, the Department of Employment's base line below which rates are classified as 'low pay' ones.

The signal workers' dispute of the summer of 1994 illustrated the shameful state of railway pay for both skilled and unskilled staff. The increased productivity of signals staff was revealed by the fact that the numbers employed had declined from 6,695 in

1984 to 4,600 in 1994, a reduction due primarily to the replacement of manually operated signals by electronically controlled ones. And yet the rate of pay for the lowest grade of signalman/signalwoman who nevertheless required skill for the job, was £146 a week, or below the £150.30 paid a station cleaner.[19]

Chapter Two: **Notes**

1. British Railways Board, <u>Annual Report and Accounts</u>, 1990-91, pp.1, 34
2. Ibid., p.34
3. Commons <u>Hansard</u>, 6th ser. vol.216, 11 January 1993, col.532.
4. University of Leeds/British Railways Board, <u>A Comparative Study of European Rail Performance</u> (1979), § 6.16 p.52.
5. Department of Transport, Transport Statistic Great Britain, 1994, Table 8.5 p.171; BRB <u>Annual Report and Accounts</u>, 1994-5, p.73. House of Commons Transport Committee, Fourth Report, <u>Railway Finances</u>, vol.1, 5 July 1995, § 73 p.XXVI.
6. BRB <u>Annual Reports and Accounts</u>, 1994-5, International Performance Indicators, p.71.
7. <u>A comparative Study of European Rail Performance</u>, p.108.
8. By the Channel Tunnel Act of 1987 future British governments were precluded from investing any public money in the project. House of Commons Transport Committee, Fourth Report, <u>Railway Finances</u>, § 19 p.XI.
9. <u>Transport Review</u>, 11 April 1980, p.6.
10. Central Rail Users' Consultative Committee, <u>Annual Report</u>, 1994-5, pp.5-6.
11. <u>Railway Finances</u>, (1995), Table 5 p.XXIX
12. Railway Industries Association, evidence to the Transport Committee, Ibid, § 93 p.XXXI.
13. Ibid., § 94 p.XXXII.
14. Ibid., § 98 p.XXXIV.
15. Idem.
16. British Railways Board, <u>Annual Report and Accounts</u>, 1994-95, p.7.
17. British Railways Board, <u>Annual Reports and Accounts</u>.
18. <u>Transport Review</u>, 29 January 1988.
19. <u>The Observer</u>, 26 June 1994, citing two Railtrack job advertisements.

Chapter Three
The Motor Car:
Liberator or Menace

1996 marks the centenary of the repeal of the 1865 Locomotives and Roads Act – the Red Flag Law – which limited the speed of mechanically propelled vehicles on country roads to four miles an hour and on town streets to two miles an hour, and directed that they should be preceded at sixty yards by a person carrying a red flag. The Act was designed to control the use of steam tractors or locomotives but was later used to regulate the use of petrol driven motor cars. By 1896 it had largely become unenforceable and a dead letter; but the few hundred motorists in Britain at the time hailed the repeal as an important step forward in the progress to greater mobility.

Early motorists were often viewed with considerable class resentment. With few exceptions they were members of the idle rich:

> Early motor cars were seen as outward signs of privilege, making a terrible clatter, giving off malodorous smells, dropping oil everywhere – not to mention leaving great clouds of dust in their wake – which caused people to jump for safety and run for shelter. They frightened the horses too, and caused dreadful accidents.[1]

Early motor cars were works of craftsmanship, individually produced in small numbers for a very limited market. The first motor manufacturing companies were often established in disused warehouses or workshops. Firms such as Daimler, Aston-Martin and Rover produced annually no more than a few hundred vehicles whose high prices put them well beyond the means of all but the wealthiest members of society.[2]

This pattern of development was changed in the decade before the outbreak of World War I with the introduction of American methods of production into the British scene. Henry Ford's first production of his famous Model T came in the USA in 1908. In 1911 he opened a factory at Trafford Park, Manchester, which remained his headquarters in Britain until 1931 when production was moved to Dagenham in Essex. The well-known methods of the moving assembly line, where the components were brought to the workers by overhead delivery; standardised components and interchangeable parts, made successive reductions in price and a vast extension of the market possible. By 1914 the Ford 'Runabout', with a low horse-power engine, was selling at the remarkably low price of £125. The pace of work at Old Trafford, and then Dagenham, was relentless, but, by the standards of the time, the hours of work, at 48 per week, were low, and wages, at £3 a week, were high. Assembly line workers were encouraged to buy one of the cars they helped to produce, and this stimulated the spread of ownership to better paid workers in the UK, a trend which was farther encouraged by the production of the first 'baby' cars by the firms of Singer and Rover in 1912. Even so, car ownership was generally limited to the better-off classes for at least a further four decades.

Between 1912 and 1914 there was a boom in the production of cyclecars, low-powered motor vehicles akin to motor cycles, and selling generally at less than £ 100. Even the most popular of these, the Humberette, offered cheap motoring but 'at the cost of a sacrifice of power and space'.

In the decade before the outbreak of World War I the number of private cars in Britain rose from a mere 16,000 in 1905 to 132,000 in 1914, when the 124,000 motor cycles were nearly as numerous.[3] The development of motorised freight transport came far more slowly, largely for technical reasons. While horse-drawn passenger transport fell in the ten years to 1914, horse-drawn freight traffic grew. Even as late as 1924 the number of horse-drawn freight vehicles on the roads was 374,000, not many fewer than had been the case as early as 1881.[4]

World War I, however, had the long run influence of boosting the motor vehicle industry. Though most car manufacturing firms, such as Morris and Singer, concentrated on munitions production, a few privileged firms, such as Austin, were busy producing trucks for the War Department; the manufacture of aero engines by such firms as Napier, Rolls-Royce and Sunbeam, provided valuable experience in advanced technology. Following the Armistice, men and women who had driven War

Department trucks in France and further afield, took advantage of buying such vehicles at knockdown prices and started businesses as carriers on their own account.

In the Inter-War years the growth of passenger transport by tram, bus or private car ate into the revenues of the railways, and made it hard, and sometimes impossible, for them to declare acceptable dividends to their shareholders. It also limited the sums available for investment in electrification and much needed modernisation of freight train haulage.

Although in 1939 the railways were in difficulties, private car ownership was limited to only two million vehicles, only a tenth of the 1990 figure. It was partly due to the fact that, in 1945, the railways were in such a poor state of organisation and technological development that they failed to retain a larger proportion of long distance transport in passengers and goods.

The explosion in the number and use of road motor vehicles came from about the mid 1950s. Several years of virtually full employment after 1945, the end of petrol rationing in 1952 and the ending of the British Transport Commission's involvement in road freight transport under the terms of the Transport Act of 1953 – which abolished the Road Transport Executive and 'liberated' the freight haulage side of the motor transport industry – all encouraged this boom.

However, it would be misleading to attribute the rapid expansion in the number of road passenger and freight vehicles solely, or even largely, to government policies. In 1960, when the Ministry of Transport set up a study group under Colin Buchanan to consider

the long term development of roads and traffic in urban areas and their influence on urban development,

the committee produced some startling conclusions. The Buchanan Report, Traffic in Towns, published in 1963, noted that

the population appears to be as intent on owning cars as the manufacturers are in meeting demand.[5]

The opinion of the Committee's Steering Group was every bit as decisive:

There is no doubt that the desire to own a car is both widespread and intense. The number of people who genuinely do not desire to possess their own private means of transport must be very small.[6]

The Committee had the foresight to recognise the potential dangers of the traffic trends of their time. The Steering Group, in the final paragraph of its statement, warned:

> We are nourishing at immense cost a monster of great potential destructiveness. And yet we love him dearly. Regarded in the collective aspect as 'the traffic problem', the motor car is clearly a menace which can spoil our civilisation. But translated into the terms of the vehicle that stands in our garage (or more often ... is parked outside our door or, more commonly, outside someone else's door) we regard it as one of our most treasured possessions or dearest ambitions, an immense convenience, an expander of the dimensions of life, an instrument of emancipation, a symbol of the modern age.[7]

Nevertheless, two influences in particular were artificially boosting car ownership in the years to 1996, the Transport Act of 1985 and the rapid increase in the number of company cars. Under the Transport Act 1985 bus services outside London were deregulated, resulting in the provision of passenger services being dictated by considerations of profit and loss – except in cases where local or central government provided subsidies for operations based on social need. In the years following deregulation, the number of passenger journeys by bus, outside the London area, fell from 4,488 million in 1984 – the last year before deregulation – to 3,354 million in 1992-3, a drop of approximately one third. Bus services tended to become plentiful in the peak hours of travel but very sparse at off-peak times. Many thousands of citizens living in remote areas of the country faced the stark alternatives at those times of investing in a car – if they could afford it – or staying at home.[8]

More important is the growth in the number of company cars. These rose from 560,000 in 1978, the year before Margaret Thatcher became Prime Minister, to two million in 1990, or by five times. For a minority of owners of these vehicles the car is essential to the job, but for the large majority the car is largely a perk. Adam Raphael estimated in 1990 that a Vauxhall Cavalier, used solely for 12,000 miles of private motoring, was worth the equivalent of a salary increase of £3,300. The cost to the employer, however, was only 40-80 per cent of the benefit, partly because tax on the National Insurance was being avoided. A company car is a very efficient form of tax avoidance as well as being a much prized status symbol. It is also a well established perk which goes with managerial and executive office.[9]

Surveying developments in the thirty years following the publication of the Buchanan Report three features are outstanding. These are the economic costs of traffic congestion: the effects on the nation's health, particularly the health of urban children and older citizens, and the social costs which result from the disruption of urban and village life.

The number of motor vehicles on Britain's roads rose from just over two million cars and 418,000 motor cycles in August 1939 through 14 million cars and 1¼ million motor cycles in 1979 to 25 million cars, and a decline to 700,000 in the number of motor cycles in 1996. With road space growing at a slower pace than the number of motor vehicles a problem of congestion was bound to arise. Buchanan had considered overcrowding in urban roads; by 1989 two reports, the CBI's Trade Routes to the Future and the Institution of Civil Engineers' Congestion, examined the characteristics and costs of congestion nationally. The CBI estimated the total cost to be £15 billion annually.[10] It stressed the importance of expanding the motorway and trunk road network and on capitalising on the opportunities for rail. The ICE report pointed to the cost of delays and unreliability, the loss of efficiencies through unpredictable travel times, environmental damage and personal stress. Both reports advocated measures to switch traffic from road to rail.

The first report of the Royal Commission on Environmental Pollution, published as early as February 1971, warned that the forecast doubling of the number of motor vehicles on the roads by 1995 would possibly lead to the deterioration of air quality in areas of heavy road transport.[11] The Commission's fourth report: Pollution Control: Progress and Problems, (1974), observed both that 'it was becoming increasingly apparent' that it would not be possible 'to cater for the unrestricted use [of vehicles] without engineering works on a scale that would be socially unacceptable' and that 'limitation in the use of motor vehicles would be imposed in order to safeguard the local environment'. Such measures would 'lead to a reduction not only of their exhaust gases, but also of their noise![12]

By the time of the 18th report of the Commission, entitled Transport and the Environment, (October 1994), there was a wealth of evidence to link the increase in the volume of motor vehicle pollutants with the incidence of nasal, lung and heart diseases. Since 1983 there had been a fivefold increase in the number of families in the UK applying for disability grants because their children had severe asthma.[13] When the Labour MP Mr Denham pointed out in the House of Commons on 18th July 1994 that a million sufferers were at risk from air pollution and challenged the Secretary of State for Transport, John MacGregor, with complacency, the minister claimed in reply that the spread of catalytic converters in motor vehicles would reduce harmful emissions by 75 per cent.[14]

John MacGregor was too complacent. Transport and the Environment noted:

> Catalytic converters operate only after they have reached a certain temperature; when an engine has been started from cold, and emissions are highest, the exhaust gases take some time to reach this temperature, and they may drop below it again if the engine is idling.
> A high proportion of car trips are too short for catalytic converters to achieve efficient operation.[15]

The test cycle of UK petrol driven vehicles is eleven kilometers, carried out at a temperature of 20-30°C, and emissions are not measured during the first forty seconds – the most polluting ones – of the engine's running. Thus the impression given by the Department of Transport of the air-purifying effects of catalytic converters is over-sanguine.

Diesel powered cars and trucks now constitute nearly a quarter of the vehicles on Britain's roads.[16] Heavy diesel trucks and diesel cars can generally meet present emission limits without pollution control devices being fitted to their exhausts.

This is due to advances in engine technology, such as turbo-charging, intercooling and electronic injection; but they cannot eliminate particulates which are defined as a wide range of solid and liquid particles in the air which arise from the combustion process in the motor engine. Particulate traps may have to be fitted to burn off the trapped particulates, but these traps are too bulky to be fitted into smaller vehicles. To work properly they require a high-temperature engine, but these temperatures cause an increase in the amounts of toxic gases, especially nitrogen oxides, which are emitted from the exhaust.[17] Until very recently the government encouraged the switch, by tax con-cessions, to diesel as less polluting than petrol.

Thus, technological improvements in the i.c. engine and in catalytic converters may reduce air pollution from motor vehicles by up to 75 per cent in the short run. In the longer run, if the headlong increase in the use of the car is not checked, the absolute amount of air pollution may well increase.

Even though the damaging effects of vehicle exhausts are checked, the environmental effects are likely to remain. As early as 1970 John Tetlow and Anthony Goss deplored the fact that

> towns as places to live in have been sacrificed to the
> traffic. Quiet residential streets have been turned into
> major one-way traffic arteries. A proliferation of street
> furniture – signs, signals, symbols, flashing lights,
> meters, white and yellow paint – these are the 'solution'
> being administered.[18]

Since they wrote, an attempt has been made to mitigate the effects of traffic in towns by the construction of by-passes. But where there are houses and shops transport needs are generated. New street furniture, especially pavement bollards to prevent on-pavement parking, have appeared on the scene.

More seriously, community life is disrupted through potentially dangerous traffic flows, making it harder for residents on one side of the street to meet up with those on the other side. Street parties and celebrations among neighbours were far more numerous on VE Day in 1945 than they were on the Day's fiftieth anniversary in 1995.

Many of those living in communities experiencing heavy road traffic flows consider that the harmful effects of the noise from the vehicles is more damaging to health than the fumes from exhausts. A study of thirteen OECD countries suggested that between 7 and 31 per cent of the populations were exposed to traffic noise above the 'acceptable' level of 65 decibels, compared to between 0.4 and 4.0 per cent of noise from railways. For a given amount of freight moved or number of passengers carried at the same speed rail is on average 5 to 10 decibels quieter than road.[19] It is only recently beginning to be understood how serious is the damage to hearing being caused by excessive noise. There is not only the phenomenon of increasing deafness, but also the increase in tinnitus – the presence of ringing or other noise in the ear or ears. According to the Institute of Hearing Research there are about four million sufferers from tinnitus in the UK.[20] It would be misleading to claim that such a large incidence of the disease was entirely due to excessive noise since the age of the sufferer plays a large part; but this does not undermine the case for reducing to the utmost noise that arises from vehicle movements and switching traffic from road to rail where possible.

The exponents of laissez-faire maintain that the solution of the environment problems arising from the gigantic growth of motorised transport, the pollution of the atmosphere and the increasing noise can best be left to market forces. They maintain that it will be in the economic interest of car manufacturers to refine the production of catalytic converters to such an extent that not only will it be possible to eliminate damaging fumes but also their substitution by pleasant odours can be created.

Similarly, truck manufacturers would find it worth their while to reduce to the utmost the amount of noise generated by their vehicles. However, the economist Frances Cairncross, who has experienced and studied the environmental problems of the traffic of Los Angeles, answered the question 'Why do governments need to intervene at all?' by answering that

in environmental affairs the invisible hand of the market fails to align the interests of the individual or the individual company with those of society at large.[21]

That is why it is necessary, in Part II of this book, to discover how and why the undue emphasis on motor transport, as compared with rail and water, came about, and to suggest, in Part III, how the imbalance might be rectified.

Chapter Three: Notes

1. T.C. Barker, review of J.P. Bardoo, J. Chanason and J.M. Lausc, The Automobile Revolution (1982), in The Times Literary Supplement, 15 October, 1982. See also: T.C. Barker (ed.), The Economic and Social Effects of the Spread of Motor Vehicles, (1987).
2. K. Richardson, The British Motor Industry, 1896-1939, (1977), chap.2.
3. B.R.Mitchell, Abstract of British Historical Statistics, (1962), p.230.
4. F.L.M. Thompson, 'Nineteenth Century Horse Sense', Economic History Review, 2nd ser. XXIX (1976), pp. 60-81.
5. Buchanan Report, Traffic in Towns, (1963), § 51.
6. Ibid., §§ 7 and 55.
7. Ibid.
8. Adam Raphael, 'Company Cars: the hidden cost to Britain', The Observer, 7 January 1990.
9. Transport Statistics, Great Britain, 1994 edition, Table 5.2 p.111.
10. CBI Trade Routes to the future (1989) § 28 p.13.
11. Cmnd 4585 §§ 70-1 and chap. 5.
12. Cmnd 5780 §§ 48-50.
13. Cmnd 2674 § 3.23 p.30.
14. Commons Hansard, 6th ser. vol.247, 18 July 1994, cols.10-11.
15. Transport and the Environment, §§ 8.5 and 8.6 p.120.
16. Ashden Trust (8 author symposium), How vehicle pollution affects our health, especially M. Fergusson, 'Is vehicle pollution likely to get worse?' p.21, (1994).
17. Transport and the Environment, § 8.13.
18. John Tetlow and Anthony Goss, Homes, Towns and Traffic, (1970), p.73.
19. TEST, Wrong side of the Tracks: impacts of road and rail transport on the environment, (1991), p.138.
20. Mark Anderson, 'Sound and Fury' in The Guardian: Society, 23 August 1995.
21. Francess Cairncross, Costing the Earth, (1991), p.89.

Chapter Four
Road Accidents

If an epidemic struck a British city and caused the death of more than 21,000 people in five years the disaster would have been the subject of innumerable newspaper headlines and many radio and TV programmes; and yet the death of 21,478 people on British roads in the years 1990-94 inclusive, attracted remarkably little media attention.[1] But it was not only the deaths which were appalling. Over the same five years 1,563,000 persons were injured and of these 213,470 were classed as seriously injured, many with loss of limbs and many incapacitated for life.[2] The number of persons killed on British roads in 1964 was 7,820. By 1994 it had fallen to 3,650, or by roughly half, though in the interim the number of motor vehicles on the roads had doubled. In the same period the number of injuries fell from 385,000 to 315,000, or by about one fifth. This brought the British figure below that of a number of EC countries, though the reduction in the number of child deaths was less impressive than were the achievements in the Netherlands, Denmark and Sweden.[3] Overall it was a substantial achievement for the Department of Transport and other agencies which played a part in the reduction in road accident casualties.

So why is it that this continuous slaughter largely escapes public attention? Recently, A.W. Evans, Professor of Transport Safety at University College and Imperial College, London, gave as the principal reason that between 1969 and 1994, major accidents – defined as those involving the deaths of ten or more persons – only happened ten times, although during this period there was a total of 141,000 deaths on British roads.[4] In the vast majority of cases of fatal road accidents only a few persons are involved, whether such persons are pedestrians, motorists, pedal cyclists or motor cyclists. Deaths in these circumstances are not newsworthy items. Only in two sorts of cases is media attention given; where large numbers of pedestrians or multi-passenger-carrying vehicles are involved. As an example of the first of these kinds of cases there was a disaster on a badly lit Chatham road early in the evening of 4 December 1951, when a marching squad of 52 Royal Marine cadets was run into from behind by a bus which killed 24 of them. This was described by the following day's Times as the most serious road accident that had so far occurred on British roads. As an example of the second kind, 32 occupants of a coach travelling from Pately Bridge to Grassington on 27 May 1975 were killed when the vehicle went out of control on a sharp bend in the road, crashed through a barrier and turned on its roof.[5] This was a very exceptional circumstance which did attract the news headlines. Bus or coach travel is the safest form of transport by road;[6] yet because they read newspaper reports of the very occasional serious accidents involving a bus or coach, potential passengers rate the risk of death by these means higher than is warranted by the statistics.

There were various reasons for the reduction in the number of road casualties. These include safety legislation; local authority regulations; changes in the types of vehicles using the roads; changes in the design and manufacture of cars and the growth in public awareness of danger through personal experience and through being informed by the media.

Until 1927 there was a free-for-all situation at traffic junctions, with many accidents occurring because of mis-judgements or misunderstandings by road users. In that year the first automatic signals were installed. Their general introduction took many years, but the change was beneficial for the reduction of road casualties. In 1930 maximum working hours were introduced for public service vehicle (PSV) drivers. Under Leslie Hore-Belisha, (Minister of Transport, 1934-37), the first Belisha beacon and Belisha crossings were introduced. During the war years 1939-45 road signposts were removed and streets were unlit, or very dimly lit. In consequence fatal road accidents rose dramatically from 6,648 in 1938, the last year of peace, to 9,169 – an all time high– in 1941.[7] The experience of wartime prompted greater attention being given to better road lighting and improved road signs when peace was restored. In 1951 1,971 pedal and motor cyclists were involved in fatal road accidents, compared with 877 drivers of four-wheeled motor vehicles. It was understandable, therefore, that there was strong public pressure for the improvement of bicycle and motor cycle brakes. However, it was not until 1973 that the wearing of safety helmets was made compulsory for motor cyclists. By 1959 the number of car occupants killed was more than double the number of cyclist victims and attention was directed to the standard of motor car maintenance. From that year on the annual testing of all motor vehicles over ten years old was made compulsory. In 1966 the fixing of seat belts was obligatory for all new cars, although it was not until 1983 that the wearing of seat belts became law for all drivers and front seat passengers. For safer driving at road intersections, mini roundabouts were introduced from 1975 onwards. In 1986 attention was directed to the equipment of heavy goods vehicles (HGVs). Close-proximity and wide-angle-view mirrors were made compulsory. In the 1990s the emphasis was on measures to curb 'road hogs' on motorways and to give priority to buses in large towns and cities by the introduction of red routes. On motorways speed enforcement cameras were introduced, while the Traffic Calming Act, 1992, resulted in an increasing number of road humps, textured and coloured road surfaces and chicanes.[8] In Oxfordshire, after such schemes had been in force for over a year, it was reported that there had been a reduction of 59 per cent in all accidents.[9] The most recent innovation was the reduction in speed limits from 70 to 50 mph on certain congested motorways to even out the flow of traffic, reduce congestion and atmospheric pollution and, paradoxically, to reduce journey times. The first experimental adoption of this policy took place on a congested stretch of the M25 in the summer of 1995.

Through such organisations as the Road Research Laboratory, the Motor Industry Research Association, and the Research Group of the Birmingham Accident Hospital, efforts have been made to make the design of motor vehicles more conducive to accident prevention. Among the improvements they have advocated, and which have been widely adopted, are the provision of a better forward view for drivers by manufacturing bonnets and mudguards to slope downwards, enabling young children to be seen more easily; the installation of more flexible side mirrors and the avoidance of sharp edges on the exteriors of vehicles.[10] However, the introduction of these improvements cost money and should therefore be introduced by legislation; otherwise the 'rogue' carrier or manufacturer, influenced by market forces, may well fail to comply with the best safety standards. The road freight industry is indeed highly competitive; the 237 inspectors of the Vehicle Inspectorate Agency issued 11,996 prohibition notices to owners of heavy goods vehicles between April and September 1994 for allowing their vehicles to be driven on the roads in an unsafe mechanical condition. Over the same period of time the 166 traffic examiners, working by the roadside, stopped 2,658 HGV drivers from being on the road overloaded or with insecure consignments.[11]

So, are HGVs a menace or a blessing to other road users? The traders argue that it is better to have one 40 tonner on the roads than the equivalent in lighter vans. This is overlooking the fact that in consequence of the priority given to shortest-time deliveries many HGVs pound the motorways with under-capacity loads. Though casualties among HGV drivers are few, the number of personal injury road accidents in which they are involved is a cause for alarm. Between 1989 and 1993 in the West Midlands Police Force area there were as many as 2,216 in that area compared with 2,070 involving buses, though the number of bus journeys was far greater than the number of HGV trips.[12]

It is the size and weight differential which is of crucial importance in road accidents. That is why a collision between a heavy goods vehicle and a private car is more likely to cause casualties to the occupants of the car than the HGV. A lorry/lorry accident may lead to less serious injuries than a collision between a Rolls and a Mini.

Paul Niblett, of the Statistics Directorate of the Department of Transport, declared recently that drink-driving is 'one of the most serious and avoidable road safety problems'. This was recognised by the government and the BBC at least as long ago as 1964-5 when the first campaign against drinking and driving was launched. But throughout the next decade the loss of life remained alarmingly high. In 1979 1,650 persons died in drink-drive accidents. By 1994 the number had fallen by two thirds to

510 in the context of a general decline in the number of fatal road accidents. Nevertheless, the toll from drink-driving amounts to about one seventh of all people killed on British roads. Put another way, it is still the case that an average of ten persons die every week from this cause. A drink-drive accident occurs where one or more of the drivers or riders refuse to submit a breath test or fail either (a) a breath test by registering over 35 micro-grams of alcohol per 100 millimetres of breath or (b) a blood test by registering more than 80 milligrams of alcohol per 100 millimetres of blood. The Department of Transport figures may underestimate the seriousness of the situation since the alcohol drinker may be killed instantly in the accident. Furthermore, the figures do not include people involved in 'hit and run' accidents who may have been drinking to excess.

The Department and the media have had considerable success in the last twenty years in influencing the attitude of the public towards drinking and driving. In a survey carried out in 1979, 51 per cent of those interviewed admitted drinking and driving on at least one occasion in the previous week. By 1994 in a similar-sized sample, the number of persons making this admission had fallen to 26 per cent. Government and media propaganda influenced public opinion. Between 1979 and 1994 the proportion of people who were of the opinion that drinking and driving were 'difficult to avoid in a social context' fell from 61 per cent to 30 per cent while those who held that 'if you go out for a drink with friends, knowing you have to drive, spoils your evening' fell from 64 per cent to 49 per cent.[13] In a social group you were much less likely to be considered a 'whimp' if you drank orange instead of beer or spirits.

The increase in the maximum speed attainable with high powered cars can also increase the likelihood of fatal accidents in some circumstances. These include lawbreakers driving at well over the 70 miles an hour motorway speed limit in an attempt to escape capture, or special police trying to overtake them.[14] Generally the 70 mph limit on motorways was 'not well observed'.[15]

In 1975 the number of pedestrians killed on the roads was 2,344. By 1994 the number had fallen to 1,124, or by more than half. This improvement has been the occasion for much congratulation. However, there may yet be some cause for concern since the number of deaths may have fallen because there were fewer pedestrians. Many children are now driven to school in the family car whereas their predecessors walked. In London between 1981-5 and 1993 there was a 26 per cent reduction in pedestrian road fatalities but the number of trips on foot also fell.[16]

Attempting to determine the financial cost of fatal road accidents, as governments have done since at least 1967, is a very sensitive and hazardous undertaking. In a Road Research Laboratory Report of 1971[17] Dr R.F.F. Dawson worked on the basis of discounting the value of what a person would have consumed if he or she had lived, from the costs (police, ambulance, hospital, funeral, legal, etc.) of the accident. However, following this formula produced an embarrassing anomaly. From what Dawson called 'a strictly material point of view', society would gain when the average woman was killed in a road accident. As an 'unpaid' housewife she gave a lower discounted value for output than for consumption. So Dawson added to the costs the fairly arbitrary sum of £5,000 as the 'subjective value of life which makes all lives worth living'. This sum was meant to cover all the emotional loss to family and friends resulting from the accident. Later on a change of philosophy was accepted which greatly increased the cost of fatal accidents by using a 'gross value of output' approach in which no deduction is made for what the accident victim would have consumed had he or she lived.[18]

In 1994 Kate McMahon, of the Road Safety Division of the Department of Transport, estimated that the average total cost of a fatal accident was £784,000, per person, per year, made up of £272,690 lost output; £510 ambulance and medical treatment and £510,880 human cost. Since there were 3,650 persons killed in road accidents that year the overall cost to the nation was £28,619,285. The cost of a serious accident per person was estimated at £89,380. Since there were 45,531 of these, their cost, in total, was £40,595,607. Adding the two totals together gives a grand total of £69,214,892. Such is the high price the people of Britain have to pay for death and maiming on the roads.[19]

When weighing up the options between encouraging more use of rail transport or being satisfied with the existing level of usage of roads, the comparative accident rates of the two main means of transport are well worth considering.

The statistics reveal that, for comparable kilometres travelled, occupants of motor cars are four times as likely to be killed as are train passengers. On the other hand, bus or coach passengers are only half as likely to be killed as those who travel by train.[20] The contrast is more striking when viewed over a period of time. From 1982-92 73 passengers and 94 other people were killed in rail accidents and 13 people seriously injured. Over the same span of time 52,660 persons died in road accidents.[21] It is true that over 18,000 of these were pedestrians, some of whom were chiefly to blame for their own deaths; but even allowing for this, over 34,000 car, van, cycle or motor cycle occupants or riders were killed on the roads, and this far outstripped rail-related deaths. As John Peyton, then Minister for Transport Industries, declared on the BBC on 4 September 1973, 'The casualties which happen daily and as a matter of routine on our roads are brutal and uncivilized'. Since he spoke the numbers have been brought down; but it is still 'brutal and uncivilized' that over the last five years there were 21,478 road deaths, a circumstance that should prompt urgent consideration of means to transfer as much passenger travel and freight movement as possible from road to rail.

A feature of motor vehicle behaviour recently is intensified 'road rage' when some drivers go berserk, and even resort to violence, because of real or imagined insults from other drivers.

Chapter Four: **Notes**

1. Road Accidents Great Britain, 1994, Table 3 p.89 Road
   Accidents and accident rates: by road class and severity 1981-
   1985 average, 1987-1994.
2. A serious injury is defined as one for which a person is detained
   in hospital as an 'in patient', or any of the following injuries
   whether or not they are detained in hospital: fractures, con-
   cussion, internal injuries, crushings, severe cuts and lacer-
   ations, severe general shock requiring medical treatment,
   injuries causing death 30 or more days after the accident.
   RAGB 1994 p.5.
3. A.W. Evans, Major Road Accidents: 1946-1994, RAGB 1994
   p.33.
4. RAGB, 1994 pp.38-9.
5. Ibid,. Table 8 p.102.
6. Royal Commission on Environmental Pollution, 18th Report
   Transport and the Environment, (1994), § 4.37 p.52;
   RAGB, (1994) p.88.
7. RAGB, Ibid
8. 'Calendar of events affecting road safety', RAGB, (1994) p.6.
9. Royal Commission on Environmental Pollution, 18th Report
   § 7.25 p.102. See also, Friends of the Earth, Guide to Traffic
   Calming in Residential Areas, (1987).
10. Graham Turner, The Car Makers, (1964), Appendix A, 'Road
    Accidents and Car Design', pp.245-48.
11. Written answer by Mr Norris, Transport Minister, in reply to a
    question by Mr Walley (Labour), on 12 December 1994,
    Commons Hansard, 6th ser. vol.251, col.527.
12. Written answer by Mr Norris in reply to a question by
    Mrs Dunwoody (Labour), on 19 December 1994, Commons
    Hansard, 6th ser. vol.251, col.877.
13. The above account of drink-driving is based on Paul Niblett's
    'Drinking and Driving', RAGB (1994), pp.24-32.
14. On BBC 1's Six o'clock news on 13 September 1995 a Police
    Complaints Commission spokesman revealed that up to 30
    special police a year were killed on the roads of Britain.
15. Royal Commission on Environmental Pollution, 18th Report,
    (1994) § 12.24 p.202.
16. Ibid., § 4.39 p.54.

17. R.F.F. Dawson, Current Costs of Road Accidents in Great Britain, RRL Report LR79, (1971).
18. C. Sharp and T. Jennings, Transport and the Environment, (1976) p.132.
19. Kate McMahon, 'Valuation of Road Accidents, 1994', RAGB (1994) pp.50-5 and Richard Ackroyd, Statistics Directorate Department of Transport, 'General Review of Personal Injury Road Accidents in Great Britain in 1994', RAGB (1994).
20. Howard Collings, Statistics directorate, Department of Transport 'Comparative Accident Rates for Passengers by mode of travel – a Revisit', Department of Transport, Transport Statistics Great Britain, (1994), pp.12-16.
21. RAGB (1994) Table 2, p.88. Royal Commission on Environmental Pollution, 18th Report, § 4.36 p.52.

Chapter Five
Water and Air Transport

In 1994 a quarter of all freight movement in the UK, measured in tonne kilometres, was waterborne. The total of 52 billion tonne kilometres was nearly four times the rail contribution though only slightly less than one third of the tonne kilometres carried by road.[1] Ten years earlier the waterborne total had been a third of all freight movement, but the decline of coastwise movement of bulk fuels, principally coal and crude oil, had reduced the volume of this important component of domestic freight movement in Britain.[2] Freight carried by canal and navigable rivers forms only a small proportion of total waterborne traffic. In 1993 the tonnage lifted was only one ninth of total tonnage water-borne, and internal, i.e. canal and river, tonne kilometres represented little more than one seventh of the coastwise movements.[3]

The reasons why freight movement by canal in 1994 played such a small part in transport provision in the UK lie in the character of early canal development. When the earliest inland waterways were built in the late eighteenth and early nineteenth century they were 'essentially local affairs',[4] linking new industrial centres with their nearest navigable river or road highway and the sources of supply of their raw materials and markets for their finished products. In later years they had grown into a national system, in so far as they were joined up with one another,

> but they had never got over the stage of their being small independent and jealous units, often competing with one another, as well as with rival methods of transport such as roads ... and the horse railways. They were constructed of all sizes and shapes, and traffic passed from one to another with difficulty, and on the whole without encouragement.[5]

Because of the parochialism of their management, the canals failed to achieve a standard gauge, a situation which was the subject of adverse comment by the Parliamentary Select Committee on Railways Amalgamations as late as 1872. They lacked a George Hudson (the 'Railway King') to bludgeon them into something like a series of regional monopolies, let alone a national system. Thus, when the steam railway arrived they were in a weak bargaining position. During the years of the Railway Mania (1844-7) more than one third of canal mileage passed into railway company ownership. This was not a development that unduly disturbed canal users who often viewed the railways with favour as challengers to canal company 'monopolists'.

Parliament intended, under the Canal Carriers Act of 1845, to curb the growing monopoly power of the railway interest and to strengthen the independence of the canals. The Act encouraged the canal companies to amalgamate and to become carriers themselves, a right they had not previously enjoyed. However, this legislation was used by the railways to do the opposite – to strengthen their grip on the country's inland waterways. A railway company which acquired a canal changed its name to 'X Railway and Canal Company' and was thereby enabled to take control of other canals by purchase, lease or working agreements. Thus in the century which elapsed between the Railway Mania and railway nationalisation in 1948 a further quarter of the canal network had been acquired by the railways.

Charles Hadfield described the condition of many of those canals which came under railway control when he wrote that

> Partly by intention, partly by neglect, the general effect of high tolls, lack of dredging, closing for leisurely repairs, decaying warehouses and wharves, failure to provide or maintain cranes, and no effort to get business, was to divert trade from water to land.[6]

However, those canals which had industrial establishments on their banks and those concerns which had private basins to which coal and raw materials were delivered and from which finished products were collected, survived well into the railway age. The Birmingham Canal Navigations remained busy through the employment of 500 such basins. Though canals as long haul carriers largely disappeared, the railway often used a canal 'like a road for collection and delivery service'.[7] Where freight could be moved direct from canal barge to the railway wagon or unloaded directly from railway wagon to canal lighter, so much the better, since overall transport costs were thereby reduced.

When railways used the fact that they had acquired a monopoly position by controlling canals on a through route and overcharging their customers, there was a danger of eventual retaliatory action. In 1872 railway control of the Bridgewater Canal and high charges by the Liverpool Docks spurred investors, including Manchester Corporation, to invest in the Manchester Ship Canal, built between 1886 and 1894, to take ships of up to 12,500 tons direct from the Irish Sea to Manchester. This was by far the most important inland waterway ever built in Britain and should have encouraged greater coaster penetration into the main river estuaries.

If attention is concentrated solely on the short length of independent canals in Britain and the short haul of freight made upon them, there is a tendency to overlook the fact that freight moved by canal is only one stage of a movement which may comprise canal–railway or canal–coastal shipping transport. Historically 'transport modes complemented each other, rather than competed with each other'.[8] They still do.

In comparison with France, Germany or Spain the UK has the great advantage of a lengthy coastline in relation to its land mass. It is also blessed with some major rivers such as the Clyde, Humber, Mersey, Severn and Thames, which are navigable for many miles 'inland'. These are ideal conditions for the development of an extensive and profitable coastal trade.

The cost-structure of the coastal shipping industry has many advantages compared with that of the railways. High capital expenditure in the form of track, signalling equipment, stations and locomotives and rolling stock is essential in running a railway service. The coastal trade, whether provided by liner services performed on a fixed schedule between ports, or by 'tramps', which sail at irregular intervals whenever they have assembled a profitable cargo, has the advantage of much lower capital charges. Once the initial outlay for the purchase of the ship has been incurred, the use of the sea as 'track' is 'free', provided port dues and harbour dues have been paid.[9] The coaster is also in the position to exploit the cost advantages of the long haul. The principal elements in its costs are the charges payable at the beginning and end of the voyage and if these are spread over a lengthy mileage the cost per mile of carriage is lowered. Until railway modernisation in the middle of the present century the coaster also often had the advantage of speed of delivery. Even in the 1930s the average speed of some freight trains was 'less than one mile an hour'.[10] By contrast, the average speed of coastal liners on the very important Aberdeen–London route was fifteen miles an hour. The freight trains were delayed in transit by the absence of continuous brakes (which necessitated the stopping of the train on steep inclines and the guard's application or release of the brakes on individual wagons) and blocks at junctions due to unreliable signalling equipment.

These cost advantages of coastal shipping resulted in a bigger ton–mileage of freight being carried coastwise between 1908 and 1912 than was carried on the railways. The ton–mileage carried by coaster was over 20 billion, made up of 7 billion of coal and coke and over 13 billion for general merchandise. By contrast, the railways in the same period of time were responsible for between 13 and 15 billion tonne miles. In other words, coastal shipping performed 59 per cent of the ton–mileage compared with the 39 per cent of the railways. (The remaining two per cent was carried by canals.)[11]

This pre World War I situation in which coastal vessels took the lion's share of freight movement in Britain was significant. It was changed by the actions of German U boats and destroyers in World War I; by the actions of the UK wartime government to divert traffic to rail; and by economic depression and changes in the structure of British industry in the years that followed.

In September 1916 the German navy started unrestricted U boat warfare on British shipping. This campaign, which concentrated on the Atlantic approaches to Britain, reached a peak in April 1917 when 888,000 tons of shipping were sunk. After the convoy system was adopted for Atlantic routes in July 1917 ocean shipping losses declined, but the German navy then concentrated its attacks on ships in British coastal waters.[12] Up to this time the British government left coastal shipping industry to its own devices; but the severe losses of the second half of 1917 and the first half of 1918 caused a growing awareness of the need for control and protection of the movement of ships. Among the coastal carryings which were adversely affected by the circumstances of the war were the trade in China clay from Fowey and Poole to ports adjacent to the potteries; the traffic in slate from Caernarvon or Conway to Liverpool; cured herrings shipped from Aberdeen and Dundee to English east coast ports; steel billets and rails from Middlesborough and Barrow-in-Furness to London, and tinplate from Swansea to other ports in Wales and Southern England. In 1919 the government gave a temporary subsidy to the industry to compensate for the fact that railway freight rates were frozen 'for the duration' while coastal shipping rates rose with increasing costs, causing the coaster a loss of business because of its less favourable charges. However, when in 1918-19 the Railway Executive proved unable to move the freight (which it had been told to take over from coastal shipping) because of its shortage of wagons, there occurred a 'disease' known as 'congestion of the ports'[13] which was a powerful influence persuading the government to introduce its subsidy. This was removed in June 1919 on the promise of a reform of railway rates in the near future.

When the recovery of coastal shipping eventually took place in the inter-war years it was largely due to the industry's own efforts. The establishment of Coast Lines in Liverpool in 1917, through the merger of a number of smaller, economically weak, concerns played an important part in this recovery, based principally in the longer haul trade in bulk freight, especially in solid fuels and fuel oils. In 1923 coal formed 60 per cent of the freight carried coastwise.[14]

Nevertheless, coastal shipping had still not recovered its 1913 level of activity by 1938.[15] The recovery was impressive in the light of the rail companies' response to coastal shipping competition. Their policy of charging below cost rates for 'port to port' freight carriage, and recouping themselves from higher charges on routes where there was no coastal shipping competition, were strongly resented by Coast Lines and other coastwise shipping concerns. This policy was seen by the coasters as an attempt 'to capture the whole of the internal trade irrespective of the national advantage'.[16] During the early 1920's the impressive growth in overseas trade led the majority of the ocean port authorities to offer favourable harbour and port dues to oceangoing, as distinct from coastal, vessels. According to one critic, the failure of those authorities 'to realise the local and national advantages which would have accrued from the maintenance of coastal shipping entrances at the same rates as ocean shipping entrances', led them to neglect transshipment facilities from ocean ship to coastwise vessel.[17] This Cinderella-like treatment of the coastal trade had damaging effects on what were called the 'subsidiary' ports.

The run down of facilities for transshipment both at the oceanic ports and at the 'subsidiary' ones had serious implications for future transport policy in Britain. Given that one of the objects of future policy is to reduce congestion on the road, one of the means of achieving this would be inducing traffic to transfer to rail, but another objective could be to plan switching freight to coastal vessels. In so far as there has been a failure in the past to prevent a decline in port facilities for the coastal trade, i.e. fewer wharves, cranes and transshipment berths, the change in transport policy will be that much more difficult to attain.

The most recently released figures show that in 1994 the volume of goods carried coastwise rose by four per cent in the year to 140 million tonnes while coastal shipping movements increased by two per cent to 52 billion tonne kilometres. Crude petroleum and petrol products accounted for 82 per cent of goods moved, or 43 billion tonne kilometres.[18] This is impressive evidence of what can be achieved by moving freight by water instead of by road and should stimulate action to strengthen this environmentally friendly trend. Other freight which would be suitable for coastal transport include bulky, low value aggregates, such as sand, clay and ores. (See Fig.3.)

FIG: 3   Freight Transport by mode.

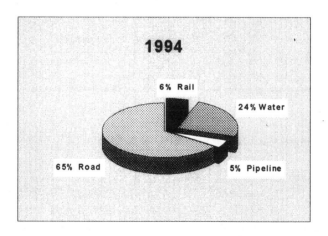

Goods moved (in millions of tonnes lifted
multiplied by distance moved)

Source: Transport Statistics Great Britain 1977-87, Table 1.13, p.27.
Ibid., 1994 edition, Table 1.13, p.43.

The big increase in the percentage of goods carried by water in
1994 is due to the growth in waterborne movements of
petroleum products.

In the second half of the twentieth century air transport played a very small part in the movement of either passengers or freight within the British Isles. In 1952 passenger travel by air measured in billion (i.e. thousand million) passenger kilometres, constituted only 0.1 per cent of total passenger travel. 41 years later, in 1993, it still carried but 0.8 per cent of those travelling.[19] The role of air transport in the movement of freight was also of little significance. Cargo lifted rose from 43,000 tons in 1964 to 59,000 tons in 1983 and 90,000 tons in 1993.[20] By contrast, freight moved by road in 1993 was 128.6 billion tons. In other words, air freight was but 1.4 per cent of that carried by road. There were twelve domestic airports listed in the UK statistics. Of these the ones with the most passenger and freight transport were linked with large international traffic, such as Heathrow, Gatwick and Manchester, or which linked England with Scotland, or Central Scotland to the Highlands, or served the link with Northern Ireland at Belfast.

Air services in Great Britain had a very tentative beginning in the years before World War I. The first operation between two points was planned for the late Summer of 1911 to mark the coronation of King George V. Between the 9th and 26th of September that year the Grahame–White Aviation Company carried mail between a primitive aerodrome at Hendon and the royal farm at Windsor. Blériot monoplanes and Farman biplanes were used for this undertaking.[21] It was a spectacular, rather than an economically based, undertaking. In the immediate post World War I years there were further interesting experiments including a scheduled service between Manchester and Blackpool via Southport. Avro Civil Aviation maintained this service between 24th May and 30th September 1919. In the following year links were established with the Channel Islands, but in 1921 all British air services ceased because of financial restraints.[22]

The industry was not firmly established in the 1920s because there was a shortage of suitable aircraft, the aerodromes were either of poor quality or were wrongly sited in relation to potential demand and there were no navigational aids. For the short-lived Channel Islands service the names of the airports were painted on aerodrome roofs as an aid for pilots. Sir Samuel Hoare who was Secretary of State for Air between 1922-4 and again from the later part of 1924 to 1929 was keen to strengthen links with the outposts of the British Empire, and to this end established Imperial Airways in 1924 through the merging of a number of struggling domestic airlines. His venture was supported with grants from the Treasury, but it did little to stimulate any further development of internal airlines. In 1927 Britain had 20 civil passenger aircraft but Germany had 167 and France 300. In the financial year 1927-8 British Government subsidies for air services were £230,000 when the German Government's counterpart was £963,000 and the French was £634,000.[23]

In 1929 the four mainline railway companies acquired powers to run air services and formed Railway Air Services (RAS) as a company. On 5 November 1934 at the annual general meeting of the RAS, Sir Eric Geddes, the Chairman, told the shareholders

> As you doubtless know, the railway companies, who suffered severely from road competition in years gone by before they had acquired powers to operate road motor services, took precautions to avoid being caught in the same way by air transport and acquired Parliamentary powers to operate air services.[24]

Oddly enough, since Sir Eric Geddes had at one time been its general manager, the LNER did not establish any air services, but the GWR, LMS and Southern Railway did so in 1934. Meanwhile in the early thirties a number of independent airlines 'flitted like brief shadows across the scene'.[25] There were far too many companies for any of them to have paid their way, and in 1938 the lines serving Scotland were merged, under pressure from the Pearson group of financial interests, into United Airways.[26]

In another merger of independent lines announced in 1935 a new company, British Airways, was created to fill the gaps in services not filled by Imperial Airways. It became the second 'chosen instrument' for Government financial support and was expected to eliminate the cut-throat competition in internal air services in Britain. Instead it placed most emphasis in developing the links with the cities of northern Europe previously so sadly neglected. Meanwhile, Railway Air Services consolidated its hold on independent operations.

None of the airline companies operating before World War II earned a profit. The government appointed Maybury Committee, in its report of 1937, deplored the wasteful competition in air services and advocated a licensing system to maintain the quality of services and restrict the number of routes being served. In 1938 the government followed some of these recommendations when establishing an Air Licensing Authority from 1 November 1938. In the same year the Air Navigation (Financial Provision) Act allocated £100,000 to help the airlines on condition that they achieved solvency within five years. However, under the Air Navigation Restriction in Time of War Order, 1939, the whole of the east side of England and part of the east of Scotland was declared a prohibited area for civil aviation. Soon after the war ended the railway owned air services came under the ownership of the Railway Executive.

Under the Civil Aviation Act of the Attlee government two state owned corporations were formed. British European Airways (BEA) was set up to run the domestic and European air services. The British Overseas Airways Corporation was also a state owned concern, though this was established by a Conservative government in 1939. BEA for most years more than paid its way on the European services but not on the domestic flights. Though there had been a considerable degree of consensus on air transport policy in the immediate post World War II years, in the early 1960s Conservative governments liberalised the licensing system under the Civil Aviation (Licensing) Act of 1960 which ended the exclusive right of the state owned corporations to operate scheduled air services. In the years that followed private companies including British United Airways (BUA) captured a large part of the charter services though BEA retained its dominance of domestic scheduled flights.

In the Thatcher administrations of 1979-90 the pace of privatisation quickened. After delays caused by the settlement of claims regarding the failed Laker Airways, British Airways, which had been an increasingly efficient and profitable business, was sold into private hands, as was the British Airports Authority.

The future prosperity of British domestic air services will depend on transport policy decisions following the General Election of 1996 or 1997. Air links to the more populous islands within Great Britain and to Northern Ireland would appear to have an assured future. But if investment is placed in high speed rail links with the Channel Tunnel, and speeds are achieved comparable with those of TGV trains in France, or those of other high speed trains in Europe, domestic air travel may well experience a relative decline. When Lyon was linked to Paris by TGV four fifths of air passenger journeys were lost.[27]

Chapter Five : **Notes**

1. Charles Bachelor's report 'Britain in Focus', Financial Times, 18 October 1995.
2. Department of the Environment, Scottish Development Department, Welsh Office, Transport Statistics Great Britain 1964-74 (1976), Table 109 p.144.
   Department of Transport, Transport Statistics Great Britain, 1994 Edition, Table 1.12, Freight Transport by Mode p.42.
3. Transport Statistics Great Britain (1994), Table 6.11 p.140.
4. Charles Hadfield, British Canals, (1950), p.180.
5. Ibid.
6. C. Hadfield, British Canals, p.187.
7. Ibid.
8. John Armstrong 'Inland Navigation and the Local Economy', in A. Kunz and J. Armstrong, Inland Navigation and Economic Development in Nineteenth Century Europe, Mainz (1995), p.307. See also the chapters by Fiona Wood and Lars U. Scholl in the same volume.
9. J. Armstrong, Freight pricing policy in coastal liner companies before the first World War, Journal of Transport History, 3rd ser. vol.10 no.2 (September 1989), p.180.
10. H.J. Dyos and D.H. Aldcroft, British Transport, (1968), p.353.

48

11. J. Armstrong, 'The Role of Coastal Shipping in UK Transport: an estimate of comparative traffic movements in 1910', Journal of Transport History, 3rd ser. vol.8 no.2 (September 1987), pp.164-170.
12. Three maps showing British merchant shipping losses 1916-18, Readers Digest, Complete Atlas of the British Isles, (1965), p.88.
13. Anon, The Coastwise Trade of the United Kingdom Past and Present, with an introduction by Sir Alfred Read (1925), p.49.
14. Ibid, p.45.
15. Dyos and Aldcroft, op.cit p.289.
16. The Coastwise Trade of the United Kingdom, p.68.
17. Ibid, p.45.
18. Charles Batchelor's report 'Britain in Focus', Financial Times, 17 October 1995.
19. Transport Statistics Great Britain 1964-74, 1976), Table 124, p.165.
20. Transport Statistics Great Britain 1994, (1994), Table 7.2, p.154.
21. John Stroud, Railway Air Services, (1987), p.9.
22. Ibid.
23. Keith Grieves, Sir Eric Geddes, (1989), p.138.
24. Stroud, op.cit. p.31.
25. This was Sir Peter Masefield's description in Journal of the Institute of Transport, vol. XXIV, March 1951, p.83.
26. A.J. Robertson, 'The new road to the Isles Highland Airways and Scottish Airways', Journal of Transport History, 3rd ser. vol.7 no.2, September 1986, pp.48-60.
27. M.P. Strohl, Europe's High Speed Trains, (1994), p.33 and chap.9 seriatim.

Chapter Six
What was wrong and what needed to be done

The information given in Part I of this book reveals that the potentialities of different means of transport outlined in Chapter One have not been realised. On the one hand railways, buses, inland waterways and coastal shipping were under-utilised while on the other the headlong growth in the number of motor vehicles outstripped the capacity of the roads to accommodate them. The result was congestion, extremely wasteful of time and money; atmospheric pollution, an increasing threat to the health particularly to the young and the old; and the visual intrusion of the car and heavy goods vehicles. The absurdity of the situation was shown in the fact that the costs of congestion and pollution together accounted for over six times more – 2 per cent – of GNP than was taken up by the railways – 0.3 per cent. (See Fig.1 p.7).

The railways of Britain were operating at less than their capacity, and the revenue they earned was often insufficient to recover their operating expenses. This was the common experience of the railways of the world. However, whereas elsewhere governments generally regarded the maintenance of an efficient railway system as necessary in the national interest, in the UK BR was under increasing pressure to act in the same way as an ordinary commercial enterprise. In an endeavour to boost revenue earned to meet the costs of operation, management raised fares and freight rates. These moves were self-defeating. Passengers and business customers were deterred from using the train and resorted increasingly to the motor vehicle. This circumstance undermined yet further the railways' chance of gaining their 'fair' share of the traffic. In the countries of the EU, railways were given more financial support to arrest their declining share of the passenger and freight markets; but the Thatcher and Major governments' rigid adherence to the doctrines of laissez-faire ensured that BR was taking a lower proportion of the UK's GNP than other European Railways did of their national products. Figure 11 on p.156 reveals that a further result of attitudes of indifference and sometimes outright hostility towards the nationalised railways was that although resources were available for basic capital maintenance, and valiant efforts were made, especially between 1989 and 1992, notably through the increased productivity of labour (see Figure 12 p.175) there were inadequate funds available for substantial further track electrification, modernisation of signalling and improvements in the safety and comfort of passenger rolling stock.

The UK government imposed strict limits on the borrowing powers of BR. The case for the Treasury banning wasteful expenditure can be understood: but restraint on investment needed to improve productivity in an essential public utility is quite another thing. The government imposed an External Financing Limit (EFL). The borrowing powers of the BR Board were defined under Section 19 of the Transport Act 1962 and Section 42 of the Transport Act 1968. In the 1980s the total borrowings were not to exceed £1,100 m. at any one time.[1] Borrowings for road construction in the 1980s and early 1990s were not subject to similar restriction.

It is arguable that in the years after 1945 the road lobby exercised a greater influence on transport policy than did the railway interest before 1921. It was not simply the British Road Federation that had such a powerful voice, but also its components such as the Society of Motor Manufacturers and Traders, The British Road Federation, the Road Haulage Association, and those bodies representing road construction interests such as the Cement and Concrete Association and the British Aggregate Construction Material Industries as well as the AA and RAC speaking for motorists, which were powerful voices in the Commons and in cabinet. They pressed for the removal or raising of the level of speed limits, for the building of more motorways and for the increase in maximum lorry weights to 24 tons in 1955, 32 tons in 1964 and to 38 tons a few months later.[2] The pre-eminence of the motor car was even reflected in the design of the bodywork. Bonnets sloped down towards the front of the car not simply as a safety measure to protect people's lives but also so that the streamlining of the vehicle would make quick acceleration and greater speed of travel possible. Some car designs were not only extra-protective to the driver and passengers but aggressive towards other cars and pedestrians. In July 1996 the Commons Transport Committee in its latest report urged the Department of Transport to

publicise the dangers caused by aggressive bull-bars in order to encourage people to remove them.[3]

There was from 1945 a growing preponderance in the Department of Transport of staff whose tasks were linked with the building of roads and the regulation of motor vehicles. Since it was the case that within the Department thousands of staff were specialists in motorways they were naturally favourable to the extension of the motorway mileage. Motorways are invaluable for good communications, but the point is that there was insufficient personnel within the department to take a more comprehensive view and put the case for alternative means of transport.

In the decade to 1996 transport economists, in many cases starting from the earlier writings of Professor A.C. Pigou whose Economics of Welfare (1920) was a trail blazer in this area, advocated the case for positive government intervention to promote public transport and reduce dependence on the car in built up areas. In 1986 Bly and Oldfield found that a policy of halving public transport fares gave a net benefit of 17 pence per additional pound spent on subsidy, while patronage increased by 16 per cent overall and car use decreased by 4 per cent[4] and Mogridge argued in favour of a combination of taxes on roads and subsidies to public transport as the best means to bring about the most efficient use of resources.[5]

A practical application of the policy of subsidising bus and underground fares to increase patronage of public transport and decrease car usage was made in London (before Bly, Oldfield and Mogridge had written) from 5 October 1981 until the Law Lords banned the Fares Fair policy on 17 December that year. Although the decision to cut fares by an average of 32 per cent was attacked from the Thatcher government benches and the London Standard, the response of Londoners was generally en-thusiastic. The new cheaper fares resulted in a 13 per cent increase in bus travel while 7 per cent more people travelled on the Underground. The decline in the use of cars, at only 2 per cent, was far less dramatic, but at least a governing party at County Hall had reversed the seemingly relentless decline in public transport use in the capital.[6]

The problems in the bus industry which needed solution were that fares were at a level to deter people who had access to private cars from switching to public transport, while in the more remote country districts at least, subsidies were needed to help cover operators' costs.

The Thatcher governments' Transport Act of 1980 deregulated the quantity control of express coaches – those with a minimum of 15 miles between stops – and the Transport Act of 1985 deregulated bus services throughout the UK outside London. When Peter R.White wrote his important account of bus deregulation in 1987 for publication in the following year he could only make provisional conclusions. These were 'that neither the worst fears nor the naive hopes of some proponents' had yet been realised.[7] However, the National Consumer Council in its October 1990 report painted a picture of poor information services and irregular changes of timetables. The Department of Transport's returns show that the number of passenger journeys in the UK fell from 6,625 million in 1978 to 5,238 in 1989.[8]

The damage to the coastal trade was done between 1914 and 1917 when the Railway Executive Committee, as a wartime emergency measure, was subject to a freeze on its charges while the costs of coastal shipping rose with the general rise in prices and many experienced sailors were recruited into the armed forces. Furthermore, following the return to the Gold Standard in 1925 there was intense pressure from the Board of Trade on the port authorities to expand capacity for ocean going vessels. This tended to relegate the coastal trade to second class status and for the provision of adequate berthing for coastwise vessels to be neglected. Finally the railways' policy towards the coastal trade in the inter-war years was to attempt to divert traffic from coaster to freight train by charging specially reduced freight rates for 'port to port' traffic.

What the coastal trade needed, then, was a recognition of its value as an important means of switching heavy freight traffic from railway to the coastal service and expenditure by means of low interest rate loans to maintain port facilities.

There was a regrettable decline in the use of the inland waterways for the movement of freight. In the decade to 1992 the tonne-kilometres of freight carried halved – from 0.4 billion in 1982 to 0.2 billion in 1992. This contrasted unfavourably with the situation in Germany where inland waterways traffic rose from 51.7 to 57.1 billion tonne kilometres over the same span of time. The Netherlands also increased its use of inland waterways in the ten years from 30.8 to 35.7 billion tonne kilometres.[9] If governments in the United Kingdom were serious about getting heavy goods traffic off the roads there was a case for making a greater mileage of the canals suitable for freight movement.

One gratifying trend in Britain's recent transport history – though certainly no cause for complacency – has been the decline in the total of road deaths. An appalling total of 7,985 was reached in the post World War II peak of 1966. By 1993 the number killed had fallen to 3,814. In this respect the UK's record compared favourable with that of other European countries. Only the Netherlands had kept down its fatality rate to Britain's 8 per 100,000 of the population annually whereas, at the other extreme, Portugal's figure was 34 per 100,000.[10] Urgently required for further progress in this direction were measures effecting transference of passengers from private to public transport and freight from heavy goods vehicles on the roads to rail and waterway transport.

Perhaps the most striking change in the British transport scene since 1945 was the dramatic fall in the use of pedal cycles. In 1949 the distances travelled by cyclists were just over half those of people travelling in cars – 23.6 billion vehicle kilometres compared with 46.5 billion kilometres. By 1993 road travellers were more than nine times as likely to be travelling by car than by pedal cycle. (The figures were 4.5 billion kilometres and 410.2 billion kilometres.)[11] The reason for this dramatic collapse in cycle use was that much of the joy had gone from this means of travel, especially in built up areas. Not only were cyclists more than twelve times as likely to be killed or seriously injured than were car riders, but also the threat to health through damage to the respiratory system was far greater.

If cycling was to be made more widespread and popular, intervention by government at national and local authority level was needed to create a national system of cycleways.

Chapter Six: **Notes**

1. British Railways Board, Annual Report and Accounts 1985/86. Notes to the Accounts, Loans and Leasing Liabilities. p.49.
2. M. Hamer, Wheels within Wheels, pp.80, 81, 89.
3. Commons Transport Committee, 3rd Report, Session 1995-6, 19 June 1996, Risk Reduction for Vulnerable Road Users, III 4 Vehicles, p.XVII.
4. P. Bly and R.H. Oldfield, An Analytic Assessment of Subsidies to Bus Services, Transportation Science 20, (1986), pp.200-212.
5. M.J.H. Mogridge, Travel in Towns, (1990), p.243.
6. Transportation and Development Department, GLC, Travel Patterns in London and the effects of recent changes in London Transport fares, (April 1983), p.4.
7. Peter R. White, 'British Experience with Deregulation of Local Bus Services', in J.S. Dodgson and N. Topham (ed), Bus Deregulation and Privatisation, (1988), pp.13-43.
8. Transport Statistics Great Britain, 1979-1989, (1990), Table 2.39, p.95.
9. Transport Statistics Great Britain, 1994, Table 8.5, p.171.
10. Ibid., Table 9.4, p.182.
11. See Howard Collings, 'Comparative accident rates for passengers by mode of transport', Transport Statistics Great Britain, 1979-89, p.1 and the same author's 'Comparative accident rates for passengers by mode of travel – a Re-visit', Transport Statistics Great Britain, 1994, p.12.   See also Ibid., p.182.

Chapter Seven
Plans for a Comprehensive
Transport Policy Thwarted

As Prime Minister of the war-time Coalition government from
6 December 1916, David Lloyd George called upon dis-
tinguished leaders in business to undertake special tasks arising
from the prosecution of the war. The North Eastern Railway
Company was recognised as one of the most efficiently run in
Britain and this distinction was attributed to the company's
General Manager of the Traffic Department, Sir Eric Geddes. In
the summer of 1916 Lloyd George's major concern was the
inadequate supply of shells for the artillery, positioned at
20 yards intervals behind the front line trenches occupied by the
infantry. The fear on the allied side was that the bombardment of
the enemy lines, before what became known as the Battle of the
Somme, would be inadequate, and that the counter offensive by
the German forces would inflict more casualties on the British
and French than they had inflicted on the Germans. In the event
this is what happened. The British troops suffered dispro-
portionately heavy casualties, mainly because of the poor state
of transport in France and at the ports on both sides of the
English Channel. Lloyd George tried to persuade Field Marshall
Lord Kitchener to send a mission of experts to examine the
situation and make recommendations; but before this could
happen Kitchener was drowned when HMS Hampshire struck a
mine off the Orkneys on 5 June 1916. On the day that Kitchener's
death was reported in the press Lloyd George asked Geddes, 'If
I go, will you go and put transport right in France?' Geddes
agreed and in September that year the Premier appointed him
Director General of Military Railways at the War Office.
Because of concern in the military hierarchy of a civilian being
placed in such an important post, Geddes was given the
honorary rank of Major General.[1]

On his arrival in France Geddes surveyed the transport
situation and reported back to Lloyd George:

The troops were fagged out because of lack of transport. The railheads were ten to fifteen miles back. The roads were blocked and gun ammunition and guns were piling up in England. The transport network was so heavily sectionalised that responsible officers had a narrow focus on problems, which enabled them to make slight adjustments, but not to tackle the larger problems. Road, railway and port facilities were organised separately, rather than interdependently, so no reviews of the complete service occurred and planning took place in pennyworths.[2]

In that last vital 15 mile chain of communications to the front line the roads were a quagmire and there was an inadequate number of road stones to repair them. Geddes supervised the construction of light railways to fill the gap. More importantly, from the long term point of view, his experience in France gave him an understanding of the inter-dependence of all forms of transport and a realisation of the need for an overriding authority that could see problems 'in the round'.

Following the signing of the Armistice on 11 November 1918, the Coalition cabinet decided to call a general election less than five weeks later, on 14 December 1918. In its election manifesto the revival of the rural economy of Britain was stressed. As part of this revival —

A systematic improvement of transport in the agricultural areas must form an essential part of every scheme for the development of the resources of the soil, and the government are preparing plans with a view to increasing these facilities on a large scale.[3]

The overwhelming majority of those who were given the Lloyd George/Bonar Law Coalition 'coupon' and were elected were Tories determined to make a bonfire of government ownership and controls. As Geddes wrote in a letter to Lloyd George on 13 March 1919:

If you scrape the whitewash of progress off 90 per cent of the Coalitionists, they are hard shelled Tories still, and unless we are going to get blocked, they have either to be converted or reverted.[4]

On 10 January 1919 Geddes was appointed Minister without
Portfolio and by the end of that month he had severed his
connection with the NER in order to concentrate on producing a
Bill for the creation of a government department to be
responsible for transport as a means, inter alia, of reviving the
rural and industrial economy as foreshadowed in the election
manifesto.

The Ministry of Ways and Communications Bill which
Geddes was largely instrumental in producing, proposed that a
new department of government should control (but not own,
unless matters were so arranged by Orders in Council) railways,
canals, docks and harbours, railway-owned steam vessels, roads
and road transport, light railways and tramways, electric power
supply, mercantile marine and navigation and aerial transport.
The Bill stated that no one sectional interest should be embraced
but the national interest should be paramount and wasteful
competition should be avoided.

The draft Bill was considered by a cabinet meeting, presided
over by Lloyd George on 19 February 1919.[5] In addition to the
Geddes' proposals members had before them memoranda
including various points of major criticism of its contents. Sir
Albert Stanley, President of the Board of Trade, argued that it
would be wrong to put under the control of one ministry
competing transport services. He said 'It should be a Ministry of
Railways'. He further maintained that 'a department which was
administratively and financially responsible for one form of
transport would not be regarded as an impartial regulator of a
competing private service'. The inclusion of merchant shipping
under Clause 2(i) was an anomaly, as all other aspects of the
Bill dealt with inland transport. In an endeavour to reassure him
Geddes said that there was no provision for taking over anything
but the existing powers of the Board of Trade. Walter Long, the
First Lord of the Admiralty, took the side of Stanley. He
declared that the chances of the Bill would be greatly imperilled
by the inclusion of this clause: 'There was no vested interest in
the House of Commons so powerful as the shipping interest'.
Though his wartime experience had persuaded him that the
control of shipping was essential for smooth traffic co-

ordination, Geddes gave way to the pressure and agreed to the exclusion of the clause from the Bill. Stanley then drew attention to the proposal in the Bill to give power to the minister to take over the coasting trade. Traders would have strong objection to this provision since something between a third and a half of railway rates were more or less affected by the coasting trade, and in that way 'the coasting trade was a great regulator of rates'. The cabinet then agreed that Clause 2(i), which concerned the coasting trade, should be excluded.

The cabinet next considered a memorandum from Sir Herbert Llewelyn-Smith of the Board of Trade[6] which opposed the taking over of harbours and ports by the new ministry on the grounds that difficulty might be experienced from leading port authorities, particularly Liverpool, London and Glasgow. At this point in the discussion Geddes stood firm. His experience of the blockage of supplies in English and French ports in 1917 convinced him of the need for authoritative control. He declared:

The control of docks influenced the whole system of transport and he regarded it as a vital matter to be able to regulate traffic in the ports.

The cabinet decided that Clause 2(i)F which concerned harbours and docks should stand.

The proposal to include the electrical supply industry as the responsibility of the new ministry was dropped when Sir Herbert Llewelyn-Smith pointed out that a Bill for the Board to control the industry was already in draft. From the chair Lloyd George advocated making the railways state property since, if this was done, 'it would be much easier to deal with the menacing industrial trouble'. He could argue with railway union leaders, such as J.H. Thomas, that if they pushed their demands to the point of a strike, they would be damaging their own interest. However, he did not propose an immediate Bill to nationalise the railways. Instead 'the powers would have to be exercised by Orders in Council which would lie on the table of the House and could not be made effective without the sanction of the House of Commons'. This statement provoked Walter Long, First Lord of the Admiralty, to warn Lloyd George (who in wartime had become accustomed to the use of Orders in Council for the exercise of policy) that 'there was nothing so unpopular in the House of Commons as legislation by Order in Council'. This tactic was therefore rejected by the Cabinet.

Further defeats of Geddes followed. Jack Seely of the Air Ministry had submitted a memorandum urging the exclusion of airways from the purview of the new ministry on the grounds that the infant industry needed breathing space to expand, unfettered by government regulation. The Cabinet agreed. In advocating the inclusion of tramways in the ambit of the new ministry Geddes maintained 'that inter-urban and suburban communication were so linked up that it would be very difficult to solve the traffic problem without acquiring the right to purchase tramways', and that 'the regulation of inter-urban tramways was an integral part of solving the housing problem'. But R. Munro, the Secretary of State for Scotland, was not convinced. Glasgow, he said, would raise 'the strongest possible exception' to the Clause 4(i)A which embodied Geddes' proposals. After Lloyd George had observed that the LCC, Birmingham, Manchester and other great towns would also be vigorously opposed, the Clause was dropped.

The much emaciated Bill was then approved by the Cabinet who forwarded it to a drafting committee of three, comprising Geddes, Albert Stanley and Edward Shortt, the Home Secretary.

By the time the Second Reading of the Bill was introduced in the Commons on 17 March 1919 the roads and motor lobbies had had time to organise opposition. In introducing the Second Reading Geddes questioned:

What is our transportation policy and who is responsible
for that policy? The answer is that there is no policy and
that no one is responsible.

For this reason the government had come to the conclusion that some measure of unified control of all systems of transportation was necessary and that it was only the state, i.e. the government, that could centrally take that position. It was necessary 'to forego the luxuries of competition, private interest and local interest, in the interest of the state'. 'In the past,' he claimed, 'private interest made for development, but now it made for colossal waste'. He cited the empty mileage run by the 700,000 privately owned railway wagons as a major manifestation of that waste. He extolled the saving which standardisation of railway equipment would bring:

> Standardisation saves ... not only in manufacturing, but in stores, in repairs and in every way, with perhaps the greatest saving the introduction of electricity into our railways' haulage.

With great fervour he declared: 'This is the cold bath that the country has got to take.'

Many of the MPs from the benches behind him were not prepared to undergo the rigours of such a Spartan regimen. George Balfour, a former President of the Board of Trade, reminded members that their mandate was to quickly re-settle the country after the disturbance of war. The Bill would not help this process.[8] Lieut.Col. Buchanan, a county council member from Scotland, wanted an assurance 'that our roads, on which we pride ourselves, will not be made subservient to the railways, canals, docks, and so forth'.[9] Sir Ryland Adkins quoted the Highways Committee of the County Councils Association which demanded a separate department of the ministry to be responsible for roads. He urged the government 'to make that separate department a reality'.[10] A Liberal member, Mr. Gilbert, who served on the Select Committee on Transport, reminded the House that that Committee had recommended that the transport agencies of the country – and particularly the railways – could not be allowed to return to their pre-war position, that the temporary arrangements for the control of the railways for two years after the war would not be satisfactory as a permanent settlement and that the railways should be under unified control.[11] In summing up for the government at the end of the two days' debate Bonar Law emphasised that the country had no transport policy. It needed one. He had heard 'no suggestion of any other method of dealing with the difficult problem'.[12]

A remarkable feature of the debate were MPs' revelations that they had been subjected to an intensive lobbying campaign with letters and telegrams. Mr. Wignall, a Labour MP for the Forest of Dean, commented that he had received 'a shoal of letters and an avalanche of telegrams' every one of which asked him to vote against the Bill 'unless the roads were struck out of it'. They all came from people who owned motor cars.[13] Sir Andrew Warren confessed he had been snowed under with communications.[14] And the railwaymen's leader, J.H. Thomas, declared that there could be

'no doubt that no Bill introduced into the House has met with so much opposition – organised opposition – as this Bill has'.

The time was not far distant when a large majority of MPs had their own motor cars. Interested parties outside of the House were making use of this fact to serve their own interests as motor manufacturers and dealers and road contractors.

The pro-roads MPs tried to delay the passing of the Bill. An amendment, moved by Mr. Joynson-Hicks, that it be sent to a committee of the whole House was put, and negatived, before it was agreed that it be sent to a Standing Committee. In its further passage through Parliament the House of Lords committee on 6 August 1919 carried a proposal to leave out 'Ways and Communications' from the Bill and insert 'Transport', and that House passed the Third Reading, thus amended, on 12 August 1919.[14]

In the events of February to August 1919 Parliament missed a great opportunity. Such reforming zeal as immediately followed the Armistice, was dissipated. Geddes' aim of an integrated transport policy serving the regeneration of the nation, became a casualty in the state's retreat from the economy when confronted by the Treasury's demand for a policy of 'Back to Normalcy'. From August 1919 Transport, i.e. the railways, ceased to be regarded as an instrument of social and economic reform and were thenceforth regarded as a financial problem. Geddes was appalled by what he saw as the over-generous terms granted to the 52 independent railway companies in the years 1919-21 causing an additional charge to the Exchequer of £90 million. He was upset by constant gibes from the nascent roads lobby that his idea of a supreme transport co-ordinating body was 'impractical'.[15] In the crucial months of the early summer 1919 he lacked the immediate backing of Lloyd George who was occupied in peace negotiations in Paris. Transport questions were not discussed again in Cabinet until April 1920. Geddes chaired an economy committee which the government appointed in August 1921, influenced by an Anti Waste campaign conducted by the Daily Mail.[16] Sir Eric Geddes features in the history books on account of the Geddes Axe of economies proposed in the report of this committee, published in 10 February 1922, rather than for his infinitely more valuable attempts to overhaul transport policy. He resigned as Minister of Transport in April 1922 after less than two years in office and returned to industry where he became chairman of the Dunlop Rubber Company.

A Ministry of Transport was formed in 1919; but in the circumstances of its formation it was a misnomer. Without any control of canals, coastal shipping and airways it was not in a position adequately to integrate transport policy. In the event the new department was open to the pressure of whichever vested interest proved the strongest. This was the story of the inter-war period which will be examined in the next chapter.

Chapter Seven: Notes

1. K. Grieves, Sir Eric Geddes, Business and Government in War and Peace, (1989), p.27.
2. Ibid., p.32.
3. F.W.S. Craig, British General Election Manifestos 1900-1974, (1975), p.28.
4. K. Grieves, 'Sir Eric Geddes and the Transport Problem', Journal of Transport History, 3rd ser. vol.13, no.1, March 1992.
5. PRO War Cabinet Minutes, vol.534, Wednesday 19 February 1919.
6. PRO Memorandum, GT 6801 to War Cabinet 19 February 1919.
7. Commons Hansard, 5th ser. vol.113, cols.1763-68.
8. Ibid., col.1796.
9. Ibid., col.1830.
10. Ibid., col.1826.
11. Ibid., col.1831.
12. Ibid., col.2047.
13. Ibid., col.2910.
14. Lords, Hansard, 1919, vol.36, 12 August 1919, col.821.
15. K. Grieves, Sir Eric Geddes and the Transport Problem, Journal of Transport History, 3rd ser. vol.13, no.1, p.23, March 1992.
16. C.L. Mowat, Britain between the Wars 1918-1940, (1955), p.130.

Chapter Eight
Road versus Rail: the Struggle for Supremacy, 1919–39

Between the Armistice of 11 November 1918 and the British declaration of war against Germany on 3 September 1939 the motor industry and the railway companies jockeyed for position to have a commanding say in transport policy.[1]

In the opening years of the inter-war period the evidence pointed to the railways having the upper hand. The Railways Act of 19 August 1921 embodied most of the companies' plans for the post-war period. Before 1914 the Railway Companies Association, which had been set up in 1867, had a dominant say in determining transport policy.[2] But during the war years the companies came under government direction through the Regulation of Forces Act, 1871, and their position thereafter never reached the near-monopoly dominance of the pre-war years.

Before it sank into oblivion following the coming into operation of the Railways Act, 1921, in 1923, the Railway Companies Association had a major influence in the drafting of the terms of that Act. In 1920 the recently formed Ministry of Transport published its 'Outline of Proposals as to the future organisation of transport undertakings of Great Britain and their relation to the State.[3] On 8 December 1920 the RCA sent Sir Eric Geddes, Minister of Transport, a letter criticising the Department's proposals and including their own alternatives.[4] There were two main areas of disagreement. The Department proposed the grouping of the pre-war companies into seven organisations, including separate ones for Scotland, East Anglia and London. The RCA proposed four main groups, apart from the London area, absorbing the Scottish lines in those of the London, Midland and Scottish (LMS), and the London and North Eastern (LNER). The RCA proposals were accepted by Geddes and embodied in the Act. The other major concession exacted from the Department by the RCA concerned labour relations. The Government White Paper (Cmd 787 of 1920) proposed that the Boards of Management of each of the four main line railways should include representatives of employees,

of whom one-third might be leading administrative officials of the group, to be co-opted by the rest of the Board, and two-thirds members elected from and by the workers on the railway.

These proposals were anathema to the members of the RCA which wrote in its letter:

The Association wish to point out that such a proposal is hardly consistent with the statement made in another part of the White Paper that it is intended to hand back the railways to their owners to be managed on the basis of private enterprise as it takes from them the power of dealing with their own men or setting up their own machinery for settling disputes.

Geddes gave way to the RCA on this important point.

In the 1921 Act there was to be no worker representation on the Boards of the four main line companies. Instead, the RCA proposal that the Railway Conciliation Scheme of 1911, with Central Wages Boards consisting of an equal number of managers and men, with an appeal to a National Wages Board with four managers, four men and four users of the railway, with an impartial chairman, was revived and embodied in the Act.

As well as getting their way on the important aspects of railway organisation and management the companies were given a generous financial settlement. During the 1914-18 War and for two years after the Armistice they had been guaranteed a financial return equal to that they had earned in 1913, the last year of peace. This happened to be an exceptionally good year for both passenger and freight receipts. In addition, under Section II(1) of the Railways Act 1921, the large sum – by the standards of the time – of £60 million, spread over two years, was made available to the railway companies as compensation for the inconvenience caused to them through the period of their control by the government.

The newly created four main line companies were understandably pre-occupied in the early 1920s in developing their own organisations and were not unduly worried about other contemporary developments in the transport world. Through the Railways Act, 1921, the government transferred many of its wartime powers to the four main line private companies, though retaining some of its regulatory controls such as the obligation of the companies to act as common carriers, i.e. to accept all traffic presented to them subject to the consignees agreeing to a scale of charges previously published.

While these events were taking place the road lobby was gathering strength. The many letters and telegrams mentioned in the last chapter as having been received by MPs in protest against the proposed Ministry of Ways and Communications Bill were prompted by the Motor Legislation Committee (MLC) formed by the Automobile Association (AA) and the Society of Motor Manufacturers and Traders (SMMT) to mobilize action against the Bill. In the Commons' debate on the Bill on 18 March 1919 the chairman of the committee, William Joynson-Hicks MP, declared that 280 MPs had 'just formed a committee to promote roads' and that they were all 'gravely suspicious of roads being put under railway control'. The aims of the MLC were stated to be 'To press government to remove restrictions on the use of motor vehicles; to restore and strengthen roads and bridges and to make available enough motor fuel at reasonable prices'.

There were earlier organisations claiming to represent the interests of motorists. Harry Lawson, a motor industry financier, founded the Motor Car Club in 1896 to celebrate the repeal of the 'Red Flag' law – the Highways and Locomotives Act, 1878, which had compelled all drivers of mechanically propelled vehicles using the public roads to proceed at no more than 4 mph and to be preceded by a man walking and carrying a red flag to warn pedestrians. The secretary of Lawson's club left it in 1897 to form the Automobile Club, which was renamed the Royal Automobile Club in 1907 and has remained in being ever since. It tended to recruit the more aristocratic car-owners and has been more moderate in its legislative demands. By contrast the Automobile Association (AA) founded in 1905, was more venturesome in its early days, recruiting the 'young bloods' of the motoring community and employing traffic scouts on bicycles to spot local authority speed cops and warn their members of their presence.

The organisation agitating for improvement in the condition of the roads was the Roads Improvement Association (RIA) which was sponsored by the two cycling clubs prominent in the late nineteenth century, the Cyclists Touring Club and the National Cyclists' Union. Their widespread campaigns led to the government passing the Local Government Act in 1888 which made the counties responsible for main roads in the UK. But the most important organisation as a pressure group in the 1920s was the Society of Motor Manufacturers and Traders (SMMT) which was established in 1901 by members of the Automobile Club.

From an original membership of 21 the society grew very rapidly after the Armistice. By 1923 it had as members 200 manufacturers of commercial vehicles of all kinds; 560 manufacturers of accessories, besides firms which made agricultural tractors, tyres, etc., giving it a total membership of 1,165. This reflected an increase in the total number of registered vehicles from 24,000 in 1903 to 560,000 in 1922.[5]

The SMMT gave itself the task of organising and bringing some cohesion into a very diversified industry. In 1920 over 100 different makers of cars were included in its membership. Even as late as 1936 88 different makes were listed, of which the best known included AC, Alfa-Romeo, Alvis, Armstrong-Siddeley, Aston-Martin, Austin, Austro-Daimler, Bentley, BSA, Bugatti, Buick, Cadillac, Chevrolet, Chrysler, Crossley, Daimler, Delago, Dodge, Fiat, Ford, Fraser-Nash, Hispano-Suiza, Hudson, Humber, Invecta, etc.[6]

Car manufacturers vied with each other to secure the most alluring product names for their vehicles, names of birds and other animals being the most popular. Aspiring motorists had the choice between the Singer Bantam, the Alvis Firebird, the Riley Kestrel, or Riley Lynx or Falcon, and the Jowett Flying Fox or Jowett Kingfisher, to mention but a few. In the mid 'thirties there was a similarly impressive range in prices for the vehicles. Artisans who were car enthusiasts could afford the Singer Bantam two or four seater tourer, at £120; or possibly the cheapest Hillman at £ 295. At the other extreme were vehicles such as the Cadillac (up to £1,295); the Lincoln five passenger saloon, at £1,450, or the epitome of excellence, the Rolls-Royce Pullman limousine at £ 2,575.

Such colourful variety was tolerable enough so long as Britain's roads were not crowded; but the number of vehicles registered increased from less than one million in 1922 to three million in 1939 and problems of maintenance and repair intensified. In the US the mass-production of cars and standardisation of parts was pioneered by Henry Ford with his Model 'T' in 1908. The first Ford mass production plant set up in England was at Trafford Park, Manchester in 1911. In the 1920s it became necessary for the Ministry of Transport to standardise vehicle production to meet the demands of safety. In this task it was greatly helped by the SMMT whose Accessories and Components' Section in 1923 reported agreements reached with motor manufacturers for the standardisation of lamp brackets, brakes, rear lights, etc. As the work of the Ministry expanded to deal with these problems it recruited new staff in many cases on the recommendation of the SMMT. The two organisations became more and more intertwined. The Society's Annual Report for 1934 acknowledged this inter-dependence. It stated:

> A feature of this year's work has been a perfecting of the liaison between the Society and the various government departments. The Council is happy in having this opportunity of recording its deep sense of gratitude for the wholehearted assistance the Society has received.[7]

In May 1921, when the MLC was advocating a reduction in the Motor vehicle licence duty, since more money from vehicle licence duties was going into the Road Fund of the Treasury than was being dispersed from it for road building and maintenance, Sir Eric Geddes, Minister of Transport, agreed that the motorists had a strong case. However, Sir Otto Niemeyer, of the Treasury Department took a different view. In a letter to Sir Robert Horne, Chancellor of the Exchequer he wrote:

The interests of the Treasury are somewhat divergent from those of the Ministry of Transport. The Ministry of Transport are only concerned with the Road Fund and regard themselves naturally as the champions of the motorists, and their committee was and is a motorists' committee.[8]

Some members of the Treasury were undoubtedly far-sighted enough to see that, far from easing motor vehicle taxation, the opposite would be necessary. In October 1925 A.W. Hirst of the Treasury team minuted the Chancellor that

> competition between road and rail could only be made 'fair' by subsidizing railways or by increasing the taxation on roads. The former is clearly out of the question; and therefore the taxation on motor vehicles must be increased.[9]

Winston Churchill, who was Chancellor of the Exchequer in the Baldwin government from 1924-29, was no special friend of motorists. In the Budget of March 1926 he took some money from the Road Fund for general revenue purposes arguing that motoring was generally joyriding; a year later he took all that was left of the Road Fund surplus.[10]

The events of the General Strike of May 1926 served to allay the fears of those who considered that the motor industry had too large a grip on the Ministry of Transport. In its Annual Report the SMMT boasted:

> With the railways completely paralysed for some days, private cars, goods lorries, char-a-bancs and omnibuses were placed in their thousands at the disposal of the Authorities, and the distribution of supplies, the manning of power stations and the movement of troops were dependent entirely on them.[11]

With the rapid increase in the number of licensed road motor vehicles and the increased financial resources of the motoring organisations the four main line railway companies grew concerned at the encroachments into their revenues through motor competition. During the preparatory stages of the four Railway Road Powers Bills in 1927 the SMMT engaged in negotiations with the railways. Although, through the new legislation, the railways acquired the power to run motor bus and motor coach services, the SMMT persuaded Parliament to insert Clauses prohibiting the railways from manufacturing road motor chassis and from engaging in direct competition with municipal and other bus services.[12]

One of the main battle fields in the struggle for mastery between the motoring organisations and the railway companies was in the hearings of the Royal Commission on Transport between 1928-30. The star witness for railways was Sir Josiah Stamp, Chairman of the London Midland and Scottish Railway, who said that he 'spoke for all four main line railways'. In a hard-hitting statement he claimed that railways were treated unfairly in respect of the overhead costs they had to bear, compared with motorised road transport. He pointed out that

> the capital sunk in the purchase of land and the construction of the permanent way and in appliances for the safety of the public, and the costs of maintaining the track and equipment, and in working the signalling and other safety arrangements, together with the local rates on rail traffic

were 'necessary ingredients' in rail transport fares and rates, but that road transport through vehicle licence fees paid into the Road Fund by no means met the full cost of maintaining the roads and policing the traffic. 'Under these circumstances', he declared,

> the diversion of traffic from rail to road is artificially and unfairly stimulated and increased, and owing to this stimulus the operations of road transport are extended beyond its economic sphere.

He claimed that some of the disabilities from which the railways suffered, such as the obligation to pay passenger duty and pay the costs of road bridges over rail tracks, ought to be removed. Though he did not question the requirement that railways should publish their fares and freight rates, he was clearly riled by the fact that any upstart road haulage firm had the right to examine, free of charge, at any station or deport the lists of freight rates charged by the railway company before offering customers slightly lower charges for the same services.[13]

Speaking as a representative of 'a Conference of Motor Organisations', Sir Arthur Stanley presented a Memorandum of its members' agreed policy.[14] They maintained:

There is no just warranty for placing any portion of cost of the roads on road users, or on any one section of road users, except as a temporary expedient.

Mechanical road transport was 'differentiated for taxation from other road transport and taxed excessively'. The introduction of compulsory driving tests was 'not in the public interest' and 'all existing speed limits should be abandoned'.

Stanley was of the view that the community benefited economically far more than the users of motor vehicles themselves by the 'increased fluidity of road transport introduced by motor vehicles' and that the market should be allowed free play in the allocation of transport services between road and rail.

By 1930 the system of licensing public service vehicles was 'archaic ... being based upon Acts passed at a time when the internal combustion engine was unknown'.[15] When the Road Traffic Bill was being drafted in 1930 'representatives of the SMMT were in close touch with the Ministry of Transport throughout the many conferences and negotiations in connection with the regulations issued under the Act'. Considerable concessions and amendments in the manufacturing interests were obtained'.[16] Under the Road Traffic Act, 1930, the country was divided into eleven traffic areas, the responsibility of three traffic commissioners whose task it was to oversee the classification of vehicles, the licensing of public service vehicles and the enforcements of regulations concerning car noise and pollution and the minimum equipment of brakes and signalling devices for cars. The motoring organisations had to make concessions to the Ministry. They failed to secure the complete abolition of speed limits but 'where all wheels of a vehicle were fitted with pneumatic tyres and the vehicle was adapted to carry not more than seven persons, exclusive of the driver', it was abolished. Heavy vehicles carrying more than seven persons were made subject to a 30 mph limit. Under Section 11 there were penalties for reckless or dangerous driving and a person attempting to drive a vehicle or driving under the influence of drink was subject to a fine of £50 or imprisonment for up to four months.[17]

In 1932 a Conference under the chairmanship of Sir Arthur Salter met to consider what would be a fair basis of competition and division of function between rail and road. It concluded that road freight haulage should be subject to a licensing system. This was one of the principal features of the Road and Rail Traffic Act of 17 November 1933. Henceforward all road motor freight vehicles were obliged to hold a licence of their road worthiness and, thanks to the joint pressure of the National Union of Railwaymen (NUR) and the Transport and General Workers Union (TGWU), provide minimum conditions of service for those employed in the industry.[18] The Act introduced three kinds of hauliers' licences: 'C' licences, given to traders who carry their own goods; 'B' licences, for traders carrying partly their own goods and partly those of other traders for payment and 'A' licences, for the professional road haulier who may carry other people's goods for hire or reward (but not his or her own).[19]

After 1932 leadership in the Road lobby moved gradually from the SMMT to a new organisation, the British Road Federation (BRF) formed in that year. It grew out of a conference of motor manufacturers and the larger road construction firms called to prepare a reply to the report of the Salter conference which advocated the licensing and taxation of road lorries and trucks. It described itself at its foundation in no restrained terms, as

the one representative body which is making efforts to combat the sinister and distorted propaganda of the railways in their efforts to enslave British industry.[20]

The BRF had two kinds of members: full membership was available to firms engaged in road construction and management, such as William Cory and John Mowlem, the big road contractors; associate membership was open to owners of fleets of lorries. The SMMT continued to function but, from then on, as one of the principal organisations within the BRF.

Membership rose from 30 in 1932 to over 50 at the outbreak of World War II.

By the end of the 1920s the demands of the road lobby were different from those made at the beginning of the decade. Through the collaboration between the SMMT and the Ministry, the problem of motor vehicle regulation had been tackled and emphasis was shifted to the demand for more and better roads. From 1920 to 1930 the total expenditure on Britain's roads increased from £26.6 million to £68.5 million whilst the revenues from road taxation rose from £4.3 million to £41.0 million over the same span of time. The road contractors did very well at this time, constructing trunk roads and by-passes and improving the standards of maintenance of existing highways. However with the financial and industrial slump following the Wall Street crash both the 'National' government and the County Councils made drastic cuts in their expenditure on roads. This fell from £62,363,000 in 1931-2, to £51,881,000 in 1933-4 and led to strong protests from the BRF which sent a memorandum to every candidate in the 1935 General Election and gave increased financial support to the pro roads groups in the Commons and the Lords.[21] In the following year R. Gresham Cooke was appointed the first full-time Secretary and new and larger Headquarters were acquired at 120 Pall Mall London within easy access of Parliament. From its foundation the BRF issued a constant stream of literature advocating lower taxation of motor vehicles and increased expenditure on roads. The arts of political pressure were exercised more forcefully and cunningly than had been the case a decade earlier. Among the titles published were: Roads, Railways and Restrictions; The Case for Motor Transport and The Road and Rail Traffic Act, 1933 as it affects commercial motor users. The occasion of the beginnings of a rearmament programme in 1936 was seized upon by the organisation to send a memorandum to the Chancellor of the Exchequer. The Annual Report made clear the line that had been taken:

> It was pointed out that the new national programme for aerial armament and mechanised military equipment must depend largely on the existence of a well-

equipped British industry for the production of motor vehicles of all types. Anything which restricted the public demand for motors would have the inevitable effect of reducing the productive efficiency of the motor industry, and of its power to expand rapidly in order to meet any future national emergency.[22]

In May 1937 Herr Joachim von Ribbentrop, Hitler's Ambassador in London, accepted an invitation from the chairman and vice chairman of the AA to be elected an honorary member of the Association. It is thought that this invitation arose from the fact that both R.G. Cooke, the Secretary of the AA, and Ribbentrop were former wine salesmen. More importantly, members of all the motoring organisations had learned with interest about the German Autobahn so that, when an invitation was received from Dr Fritz Todt, the general inspector of Germany's highways to bring a party of about 200 people to inspect the German road system, the opportunity was thought too good to be missed. The Ministry of Transport considered it politically unwise to be represented in the delegation, but 58 MPs and many councillors joined the German Road Delegation (as it became known) on 24 September 1937. After being feted at the expense of the Reich the delegation reported back to Leslie Burgin, Minister of Transport, that it recommended 'that the principle of the motorway system be adopted in Britain'. This was followed up by a deputation of members of the AA, the BRF and the County Surveyors Society to the Minister in 1938 to advocate a motorway plan. On the same day Burgin met members of the parliamentary road group. He told the deputation that day that he was in favour of an experiment with a limited mileage of motor road to test motorists' and the public's reaction.[23] But the outbreak of war came before this or other like schemes could be brought to effect.

The road lobby did not have its way entirely before the outbreak of war. The railways still had their friends, including two future Prime Ministers, Anthony Eden and Harold MacMillan, to influence the decisions of the cabinet. In the thirties the railway companies endeavoured to offset their competitive disadvantages in relation to road transport by setting

up both bus and air services and in 1930 acquiring Hays Wharf
Cartage, one of the largest road transport concerns. But these
were only palliatives. In November 1938 they took the bull by
the horns and launched a 'Square Deal' campaign to try to
persuade the government to abolish all restrictions on railway
charges and 'obligations to carry', to place them on more of a
parity with road transport concerns. The proposals were
forwarded by the Ministry of Transport to the Transport
Advisory Council, a body set up under Part III of the Road and
Rail Transport Act of 1933 'to assist and advise the minister on
transport facilities generally, including co-ordination'.[24] The
railways' proposals were 'subject to many meetings and
representations by the road haulage interests'.[25] But despite this
pressure the Transport Advisory Council reported favourably on
them in April 1939. However, before legislation could be placed
on the statute book war had been declared.

Chapter Eight: **Notes**

1. UK, The Public General Acts, XI and XII Geo.V, chap.55.
2. G. Alderman, The Railway Interest, (1983), Seriatim.
3. Cmd 787 of 1920.
4. Booklet published by the GWR entitled Ministry of Transport Act,
   1920, also includes the RCA's proposals for future legislation.
   (1922).
5. SMMT, Annual Report, 1923.
6. SMMT, document of February 1936. British Library reference
   no. WP11600.
7. SMMT, Annual Report, 1934, p.7.
8. Cited in William Plowden, The Motor Car and Politics, 1896-
   1970, (1971), p.186.
9. Ibid., p.195.
10. Ibid., p.195.
11. SMMT, Annual Report, 1926, p.5.
12. SMMT, Annual Report, 1928, p.8.
13. Royal Commission on Transport, Part I, Minutes of Evidence,
    19 December 1928.

14. Ibid., in answer to question 2487.
15. Second Report of the Royal Commission on Transport:
    The Licensing and Regulation of Public Service Vehicles, 1930.
16. SMMT Annual Report, 1930, p.5.
17. Road Traffic Act, 1 August 1930.
18. P.S. Bagwell, The Railwaymen, (1963), pp.530-31.
19. Sir Gilmour Jenkins, The Ministry of Transport and Civil Aviation,
    (1959), p.104.
20. William Plowden, 'MPs and the Roads Lobby', in Anthony Barker
    and Michael Rush, The Member of Parliament and his information,
    (1970), pp.69-95.
21. British Road Federation (BRF) Annual Report (1935), pp.4-5.
22. British Road Federation (BRF) Annual Report (1936), p.5.
23. Mick Hamer, Wheels Within Wheels: a study of the road lobby,
    (1987), pp.40-44.
24. Michael Bonavia, The Four Great Railways, (1980), p.132.
    H.J. Dyos and D. Aldcroft, British Transport, (1969), pp.318-9.
25. British Road Federation, Annual Report (1939), p.10.

Chapter Nine
The Best Laid Schemes ...

Under the Attlee government's Transport Act, 1947, the second major attempt was made this century to deal with the transport problem as a whole. By 1953 the plan had been thoroughly undermined. This chapter will attempt to show how this happened and will point to the consequences for Britain's transport of this failure.

Following the Labour Party's general election defeat of 27 October 1931, a Reorganisation of Industry group of some of the party's leading specialists was established and met for the first time in March 1932. The leading London Labour politician of the day, Herbert Morrison, who had been Minister of Transport in 1929-31, was asked to prepare reports on transport and electricity. For London transport Morrison advocated a corporate form of organisation where the Board of the publicly owned industry was to be selected purely on its members' capacity. These proposals were adopted by Ramsay MacDonald's National government and embodied in the London Passenger Transport Act of 1933.[1]

Morrison's proposals that the Boards of public corporations should be composed of people chosen solely for their technical or administrative ability was challenged at the annual conferences of the Labour Party and the TUC in both 1932 and 1933. At Leicester, at the Labour Party's annual conference in October 1932, he defended his proposals for Transport and Electricity Boards as 'one of the steps on the road to socialism'. Henry Clay, of the Transport and General Workers Union, objected to the Morrisonian plan and disputed whether it would be a step towards socialism. He proposed an amendment

> that certain of the members of the National Transport Boards and/or directing or managing authority that may be established, shall be appointed only after consultation with the trade unions having members employed in the industry.

Clay argued that

the proposals which Mr Morrison puts forward 'stratify industrial society. The workers are workers and you doom them to be hewers of wood and drawers of water under the perpetual control of their bosses. They are to have no effective powers under the proposals put forward in this report. This proposal provides for an efficient bureaucracy being placed in control with no effective check on it.

Morrison rejected this proposal and replied derisively:

The Order Paper would be flooded with amendments to secure the representation of other interests ... you would run the risk of the whole show being run by dead-heads no better than the guinea pigs that now run the railway companies of Great Britain.

Since conference opinion was so divided Ernest Bevin of the Transport Workers Union suggested the reference back of the resolution and Herbert Morrison reluctantly agreed.[2]

However, in the following years' conferences Morrison got his way and Labour went on to enter the War of 1939-45 and the post-war period with his plans for authoritative corporate boards accepted for future policy making and legislation.[3]

An important reason for the success of the perky Londoner was his industriousness and his dogged persistence. Other Labour leaders seemed content to quote mere catchphrases such as 'public ownership' and 'national ownership and control' in place of careful thought and detailed study. In the early 1930s he won the argument in default of anything more convincing being put forward by a senior Labour politician of the time.

The annual TUC at Blackpool on 16 October 1944 listed railways among the few major industries 'ripe for nationalisation' and declared that the private company owners should be compensated on the basis of estimates of 'reasonable and maintainable revenue payable in government bonds'.

In the early years of the war the Department of Transport also gave thought to the form that railway ownership should take after the cessation of hostilities. In May 1940 Sir John (later Lord) Reith, the Minister of Transport, asked Sir Alfred Robinson and Dr. W.H. Coates to undertake a study of the problems of co-ordinating all forms of transport. Their report, entitled The Transport Problem in Great Britain, appeared in October 1940, and advocated the setting up of a National Transport Corporation which would

> acquire rail, road, canal and air transport, including the privately owned rail wagons and docks, and exert a greater measure of control over coastal shipping.[4]

However, when Col. J. Moore-Brabazon (later Lord Brabazon of Tara) took over as Minister of Transport on 30 October 1940, and when the Ministry changed its name to the Ministry of War Transport on 1 May 1941 and Lord Leathers replaced Brabazon, the Robinson-Coates plan was shelved. Brabazon thought the proposal was far too radical and Leathers resented any interruption with the immediate task of moving war materials,[5] though he later declared

> For the first time the country had evidence of a fully co-ordinated transport system. He doubted whether the industry would ever want to go back to the conditions prevailing before the war.[6]

Although some of the railway companies directors recognised that it would not be possible to return to the status quo after the war had ended, and the committee they appointed recommended a choice of five options, one being nationalisation, the general managers vetoed all measures of reform. In the closing months of the war the primary concern of directors and managers alike was to secure a generous financial settlement for the shareholders.[7]

The Railways of Britain had been under the control of the government-appointed Railway Executive Committee, and Lord Leathers was the Minister of War Transport responsible for their efficient operation from May 1941 to July 1945.

The general election of 5 July 1945 giving the Labour Party a large parliamentary majority gave a clear pointer to the future. In its election manifesto Let us face the Future the party promised:

> Public ownership of inland transport. Co-ordination of transport services by rail, road, air and canal cannot be achieved without unification. And unification without

public ownership means a steady struggle with
sectional interests or the enthronement by a private
monopoly which would be a menace to the rest of
industry.[8]

When the Attlee Labour government was formed in July 1945
Alfred Barnes was appointed Minister of Transport. In
policy-making influence he was but a pale shadow of Herbert
Morrison who was given the job of Lord President of the
Council with general oversight of the legislative programme. In
this capacity he made a keynote speech in the House of
Commons on 19 November 1945. It was a statement of what the
government hoped to achieve within the lifetime of one
parliament. Included in the programme were

measures designed to bring transport services, essential
to the economic well-being of the nation, under public
ownership and control. ... In regard to inland
transport, powers will be taken to bring under national
ownership the railways, canals and long distance road
services.[9]

This was taken as a 'red alert' by the road lobby. Before the
terms of the Transport Bill had been published a fierce
opposition was mobilised against the whole principle of
government ownership of road haulage. The medium for the
campaign was the Road Haulage Association (RHA), an
offshoot of the Long Distance Road Haulage Committee formed
at the time of the Royal Commission of Transport in the early
1930s. When the wartime coalition government made plans to
own a large fleet of lorries, the RHA's opposition to the scheme
was unsuccessful and the government's Road Haulage
Organisation was set up.[10] This defeat of the road lobby
strengthened its resolve to fight for the freedom of the haulier to
operate without government restraint once the war emergency
ended.

In 1945 the RHA launched what S.E. Finer has described as
a 'prophylactic campaign' against any future proposal to
nationalise road haulage[11]. At the time of the campaign's launch
the government had not published the terms of the Transport
Bill. But the Association took the view that it was better to take

'time by the forelock' and mobilise opinion against nationalisation. It was argued that once the full terms of the Bill were known and were supported by a government with a healthy majority there was little that could be done, apart from effecting minor changes.

The Transport Bill was published on 28 November 1946. It provided for the appointment of a British Transport Commission with a chairman and four other members, all appointed by the Minister. Five executive bodies were to be set up under the Transport Commission:

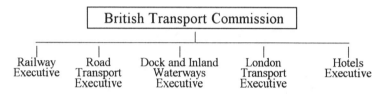

Each executive was to consist of a chairman and 4-8 members appointed by the Minister, after consultation with the Commission. The Commission was to acquire all road haulage concerns which were in 1946 predominantly engaged in long distance carriage for hire or reward under 'A' and 'B' licences, i.e. for distances of forty miles or upwards. There were to be exceptions to this provision in cases such as furniture removal or oil tankers. 'B' and 'C' licensed vehicles for owners' use were limited to a radius of twenty-five miles from base.

There was to be a Central Transport Consultative Committee for the whole of Britain assisted by Transport Users Consultative Committees for both passenger and goods traffic. The Railway Rates Tribunal of 1939 was to be replaced by a Transport Tribunal with powers to adjudicate on charges.

As soon as these provisions were known strong opposition to some of them was voiced by elements within the labour movement, by some economists and by the road lobby.

One of the most perceptive critics of the Transport Bill in the labour movement was Ernest Davies who considered that power in the Transport Commission was far too centralised for it to be able to stir the imagination and enthusiasm of the workers in the industry and the travelling public. At the time when the contents of the Bill was still under discussion, he wrote:

> The public corporation must be broken down and organised on a regional basis so that each community is aware of participation in it.

Those employed in the transport industry should feel that it was their concern

> to impart to nationalisation a greater enthusiasm among the workers than has yet been experienced, they too must be brought into the closest consultation and participation. This again requires decentralisation so that to each worker in the smallest unit the spirit of co-partnership is implanted. ... Before nationalisation can evoke in the worker a sense of ownership and participation, his status must be changed.[12]

Neither Herbert Morrison nor Alfred Barnes heeded this advice. It was not only in transport that worker representation on nationalised boards was weak or non-existent, but on all central and regional boards. In 1951 there were but 44 members possessing some previous connection with the trade union movement out of a total of some 350 members of central and regional boards of all nationalised industries.[13] Since most members of the nationalised industry boards were former directors and senior executives of the companies taken over, it is not surprising that in industrial relations the 'them and us' feeling survived. Thus, when groups hostile to public ownership attacked the Commission and its executives there was less grass roots resistance to this pressure than there might otherwise have been.

Another important criticism from the left of the transport reorganisation of 1946-8 was that over-generous compensation was being paid to the former owners of private concerns. Ernest Davies had advocated paying the railway shareholders a lump sum slightly more than the market price of their stocks. If this had been done or if the TUC formula of 1944 based on 'reasonable and maintainable revenue in the future' had been followed, the burden of compensation payments payable by the Commission would have been substantially lighter. But the Ministry of Transport was persuaded that there were greater difficulties in its implementation than there would be on the basis of compensation based on Stock Exchange prices. Initially it proposed as basis the mean of the mid-monthly quotations for the pre-election period of February-July 1945. However, Barnes was persuaded to have secret meetings with the railway company chairmen in June and September 1945 when he conceded a new settlement, a valuation based on market prices of stocks in the week 1-8 November 1946 or, where more favourable to the companies, from February-July 1945. Under this arrangement the railways were to receive £5 million more than the Ministry of Transport had proposed. The main line companies under this new valuation were to receive £907.8 million in 2½ per cent (later raised to 3 per cent) Transport Stock from the transfer date of 1 January 1948. Among other things, Barnes had been influenced by a leading article in the <u>Economist</u> of 23 November, entitled 'Nationalisation on the Cheap'.[14]

This was a complete travesty of the real situation. 1946 was an exceptionally good year for the four main line railway companies. The motor industry at that time had scarcely got into its stride with petrol rationing still in force, and only later was it in a serious position to draw business away from the railways. Furthermore, although the railway companies stock prices were at a high level they did not accurately reflect the condition of their physical assets which had deteriorated sharply during the war years. As the historian of BR noted 'there was a large backlog of repairs'.[15] The bigger millstone round the neck of the railway companies was the huge number – 653,000 – of privately owned wagons, more than half of which were over 35 years old in 1946, their fitments were of divergent patterns and their capacity was mostly ridiculously small. In the Second Reading debate on the Transport Bill, when taunted by opposition Tory MPs, Hugh Dalton, the Chancellor of the Exchequer, countered by claiming that all pre-war experience showed that before long the railways would have been on the rocks' and that 'the system was a very poor bag of physical assets'.[16]

The left-wing transport economist F. Smith compared the close attention to the structure of the executives set up under the Commission with the failure to work out the means by which the co-ordination of transport services would be achieved. He asserted that

> the one thing of fundamental importance which is never openly canvassed, either by the railways or the government, is a general plan clear and convincing, which is designed to integrate the operations and services of all forms of transport for the purpose of doing the practical job of moving persons and things from place to place with the minimum of real cost and the maximum of communal advantage. To this end it is necessary so to plan movement that the railways, inland waterways, coastal shipping and road transport, can be used each in its most appropriate functional sphere.[17]

More damaging opposition to the provision of the Transport Act and to the achievement of its purposes was inflicted by the road lobby. The circumstances of World War II brought motor transport organisations much closer to the machinery of government than was the case in World War I when horse-drawn transport still played a very significant part in the movement of war materials. After 1945 the rapid growth of peacetime motorised transport was reflected in the boom in membership and financial strength of both the RHA and the BRF. In 1945 the RHA's subscription income was £74,000 and its total assets £61,000. It had been streamlined near the end of 1944 to make it a more effective political force. In 1945 in its first annual report as a revamped organisation it noted that

> its parliamentary committee, in conjunction with the parliamentary agents and Political Adviser, is actively engaged in building up parliamentary contacts.[18]

From the date of the publication of the Transport Bill on 28 November 1946 through the six months of its passage through parliament the campaign of opposition continued in top gear, allied with the Conservative opposition in the Commons and the Lords working closely to a set of briefs prepared by the RHA.

While the RHA fought for what it saw as the interest of road hauliers, the BRF conducted a more wide-ranging campaign. Included in an imaginative set of leaflets were _An Urgent_

Message to Garage Proprietors and Motor Agents which warned its readers that

> The complete nationalisation of road haulage will be the biggest blow to you yet. Your local carrier and your local tradesmen have been good customers. A state organisation will make its own arrangement for suppliers and repairs. It's only a step from road haulage nationalisation to the state control of sales and services.

An Urgent Message to Women claimed that

> Nationalisation will mean longer queues at the shops because deliveries to the shopkeeper will be run by Civil Servants. ... Nationalisation is going to put 60,000 hauliers – little men who do a good job for you and harm no one – out of business. It might be your husband next.

There was propaganda on similar lines in An Urgent Message to the General Public, and other handouts.[19]

During J.S. Neave's period of office as part-time secretary between 1942-6 the BRF's membership of national trade associations rose dramatically from 57 to 111. By the time the Transport Bill was published it watched over the interests of more than 250,000 users of commercial road transport.[20]

Most importantly the BRF gained a sympathetic response to its case from Alfred Barnes. The Secretary of State received deputations and agreed with their members on the need for more and better roads. Speaking in the House of Commons on 6 May 1946 the Minister announced a major new road works programme to be spread over the following ten years. In its Annual Report the BRF was jubilant. 1946, it proclaimed, would be remembered as 'the year in which those who had been campaigning for a fundamental change in conception of our road system, first received official encouragement'. It also claimed that the Minister indicated 'official approval of motorways'.[21]

The significance of the BRF's friendly relations with Alfred Barnes should be seen alongside the success of its parliamentary agent, Commander Christopher Powell, in gaining recognition among MPs of his employing organisation's right to speak for road hauliers, commercial motor organisations and private motorists. The BRF's Committee of Management reported that during the Second Reading stage of the Transport Bill

the accepted authority of the Federation was amply illustrated by members of both sides of the House. During the committee stage also the Federation was frequently consulted and was able to supply information to members of the committee.[22]

It is significant that when Barnes met another BRF deputation on 23 July 1946 offering its assistance in furthering the road programme he 'welcomed the offer and invited the Federation to keep in close touch with his department'.[23] It did for many years to come during which there was no other pressure group of comparable 'clout' to counter its arguments.

Although the Tory opposition efforts, backed by the road lobby, largely failed – forty-seven separate amendments to the Bill to exempt certain types of road vehicles from the publicly owned services were all defeated – one concession made by Barnes was of vital significance. The Minister agreed to abolish the distance limit to the operation of 'C' licensed vehicles. The result was a rush of traders to obtain 'C' licences. During 1947 there was a monthly average increase in those granted of 8,606 and in 1948 the increase was much the same as traders endeavoured to control supplies and deliveries from source to destination.[24] This development thoroughly undermined the working of the Act by shifting freight movement from rail to road.

What is distressing about the story of the passage of the Transport Bill through parliament was that what influenced the decisions reached was politics, rather than economic and social policy. Dr Gourvish found 'an important and alarming element' in framing the nationalisation proposals was 'political and administrative expediency'. Discussion of the implications of the legislation for the economic operation of road and rail transport was 'conspicuously absent'.[25]

The result of the general election of 23 February 1950 was that the Labour Party was returned to power with more than a million and a quarter more votes than in 1945 but with an overall parliamentary majority of only five. On 25 October of the following year Clement Attlee asked the electorate for a new mandate and a more substantial working majority in the Commons. The outcome of the election was that Labour received its highest ever vote since the foundation of the party in 1906 – 13,948,605 – and over 200,000 more than the Conservatives, but won only 295 seats compared with its opponents' under Churchill who gained 321, and promptly formed a new administration. The Conservative election manifesto, written by Churchill, included two sentences concerning transport:

> Publicly owned rail and road transport will be organised into regional groups of workable size. Private road hauliers will be given the chance to return to business, and private lorries will no longer be crippled by the 25 mile limit.[26]

Although the victorious party's election manifesto was clear enough there were considerable problems in putting the stated aims into practice. Churchill and his cabinet team were well aware that the idea of transport co-ordination had gained some acceptance among the public. It was significant that the title given to Lord Leathers, who succeeded Alfred Barnes as Minister responsible for transport, was Secretary of State for the Co-ordination of Transport, Fuel and Power (even though his chief task was to hive off the Transport Commission's most profitable arm, the Road Transport Executive, into largely uncontrolled private ownership). It was also the case that a Gallup Poll conducted in September 1952 was by no means enthusiastic for the privatisation of British Road Services, the operational arm of the RHE. Although 48 per cent of those responding to the poll were in favour of denationalisation, 38 per cent were in favour of retaining the BRS whose supporters formed a majority in Scotland and the industrial parts of Northern England.[27] Another difficulty was that the cabinet was divided on the issue. This accounts for there being two Transport Bills, one published in July 1951 and afterwards abandoned and the second submitted to the Commons at the end of July in the same year.

The successful Bill which became law as the Transport Act 1953, provided for the abolition of the Road Haulage Executive and the sale of its property 'as quickly as is reasonably practicable'. To effect this sale a Road Haulage Disposal Board was established. The restrictions on the range of operations of road freight vehicles imposed under the Transport Act 1947 were removed. The cabinet recognised that the financial position of the BTC would be adversely affected by the obligation imposed on it to sell off its lorries at knock down prices, so the Bill provided for a Transport Levy to be paid by each road haulage licensee soon after the Bill was enacted. On 10 February 1952 the cabinet agreed by a majority not to impose a levy on long distance passenger traffic by road but was unanimous in support of a levy on road freight vehicles.[28]   On 7 October differences of opinion were revealed in cabinet on the proposal to raise a second levy on freight vehicles in 1956. Lord Leathers supported the second levy, since 'although the proposed relaxation of restrictions on railway charges might enable them to hold their own with regard to road transport for a time, the railways would in the long run be bound to suffer severely from revived competition from free road haulage'.   He had the support of the Home Secretary, Sir David Maxwell-Fyfe and of Viscount Swinton. But the Marquess of Salisbury, the Lord President of the Council, and R.A. Butler, the Chancellor of the Exchequer, were opposed so that Churchill from the chair announced that 'the balance of opinion' was against the second levy.[29]

A weakness of the Act was that it gave no practical help to coastal shipping. Although Sir Alex Lennox-Boyd, in the Second Reading debate, declared that the Coastal Shipping Advisory Council, to be established, would have the power to make recommendations on how the volume of coastal shipping might be enhanced, Mr James Callaghan (the future Prime Minister) was not satisfied. He questioned:

> How will any lessons that are arrived at by this Advisory Committee be enforced on the road haulier? ... Quite clearly they can be enforced upon the railways, which is a national undertaking, but how will the government ensure that road hauliers do not under-cut the coastal shipping rates? ... We believe that

coastwise shipping is an essential strategic need of this country.[30]

There was no positive response to James Callaghan's questions. The government could not make serious claim to be working towards the co-ordination of the different forms of transport. It is significant that the office of the Department for the Co-ordination of Transport, Fuel and Power was abolished on 3 September 1953. The Ministry of Transport and Civil Aviation took its place.

After the passing of the Transport Act, 1953, the Road Haulage Disposal Board sold off the smaller units of the Road Haulage Executive fairly quickly, but the larger concerns engaged in long distance traffic sold more slowly. The government came to the conclusion that in the national interest it would be wrong to allow these services to be broken up. Through the Transport (Disposal of Road Property) Act, 1956, it enabled the British Transport Commission to keep 15,000 of the 40,000 vehicles it had formerly held under the RHE. Thus British Road Services remained the largest and most important single road haulage concern in the country. There were also the feeder and delivery vans belonging to the railways, bringing the total up to 33,000. However, this was a very small fraction of the total of 1,200,000 road goods vehicles privately owned in 1959.[31]

The impact of the Act of 1953 on British Road Services is shown in Table 2. Up to and including 1953 the turnover and profit of BRS was increasing rapidly as traders appreciated the advantages of the 200 pooling stations of lorries, which had reduced the number of empty return journeys. The increasing profit of BRS had been the most valuable contribution to the overall finances of the BTC. After 1953 the turnover and profits of BRS shrank rapidly at the same time as the number of free road haulage concerns rose. Table 3 shows that the overall financial return of British Railways went sharply into the red from the year after the 1953 Act was passed and Table 4 shows, that the overall financial position of the Commission which showed a profit in the years 1951-53 inclusive, deteriorated rapidly after 1954.

TABLE 2 British Road Services : trading 1948-68

Year	Turnover (£m.)	Profit (£m.)	Net assets £m.)	Rate of return %	Vehicles
1948	14.3	1.1	22.9	5.2	8,208
1949	38.9	1.4	46.3	3.2	34,894
1950	62.5	−1.1	68.6	−1.6	39,932
1951	78.6	3.3	70.1	4.7	41,265
1952	77.6	1.7	72.3	2.4	39,325
1953	80.2	8.9	73.0	12.2	35,849
1954	72.7	8.7	(71.2)	(12.2)	25,442
1955	55.8	4.3	(52.8)	8.1	17,570
1956	48.5	1.8	37.7	4.8	16,377
1957	50.3	2.8	39.7	7.1	16,312
1958	49.5	2.0	42.1	4.8	15,976
1959	52.5	3.1	43.2	7.2	15,911
1960	55.5	1.8	44.2	4.1	16,184
1961	57.9	3.4	45.2	7.5	16,066
1962	60.3	3.7	45.8	8.1	16,040
1963	64.2	4.7	45.8	10.3	16,075
1964	71.1 ·	7.3	48.0	15.2	15,765
1965	79.9	7.0	64.1	11.1	18,346
1966	89.2	4.9	74.0	7.0	19,247
1967	90.7	3.0	85.0	3.7	18,210
1968	102.0	3.8	89.0	4.4	18,931

N.B. Asset figures for 1954-5 are estimates due to the fact that the Road Haulage Disposal Board, set up under the Transport Act 1953, was selling BRS road vehicles at this time. The RHE ceased to function after 1954.

Source: *National Board for Prices and Incomes Rept. No. 162: Costs, Charges and Productivity of National Freight Corporation,* App. A, Cmd 4569 of 1971.

TABLE 3 British Railways: receipts and expenditures 1948-62 (£m.)

Year	Passenger receipts	Freight receipts	Total gross receipts (incl. misc. receipts)	Total working expenses	Current operating return	Central charges allocated to railways	Overall return
1948	122.6	180.5	346.3	322.5	23.8	31.9	−8.1
1949	114.0	178.9	335.7	325.1	10.6	34.2	−23.6
1950	106.6	198.9	351.3	326.1	25.2	36.2	−11.0
1951	107.0	227.9	348.9	351.6	33.3	33.6	−0.3
1952	111.9	250.5	416.3	377.7	38.7	35.1	3.6
1953	114.8	263.1	434.7	400.1	34.6	37.4	−2.8
1954	116.6	272.8	449.3	432.9	16.4	38.3	−21.9
1955	118.1	274.2	453.9	452.1	1.8	40.1	−38.3
1956	127.5	284.1	481.0	497.5	−16.5	41.2	−57.7
1957	138.9	288.5	501.4	528.6	−27.1	41.9*	−69.0
1958	138.0	259.1	471.6	519.7	−48.1	42.6	−90.7
1959	140.0	242.7	457.4	499.4	−42.0	42.8	−84.8
1960	151.3	267.3	478.6	546.2	−67.7	45.2	−112.9
1961	157.5	236.8	474.7	561.6	−86.9	48.0	−134.9
1962	161.1	224.9	465.1	569.1	−104.0	52.1	−156.1

* From 1957 allocation does not include interest on accumulated railway losses and on new borrowing. Both these items were transferred to a special account.

Source: *Annual Reports and Accounts*, British Transport Commission.

TABLE 4 Financial Position of the British Transport Commission
1948–62

Year	Working surplus or deficit		Central charges	Surplus or deficit after central charges	Interest contained in central charges
	railways	whole under- taking			
	£m.	£m.	£m.	£m.	£m.
1948	+23.8	+40.8	45.6	–4.7	42.3
1949	+10.6	+28.1	48.8	–20.8	43.9
1950	+25.2	+37.6	51.7	–14.1	44.9
1951	+33.3	+48.1	48.0	+0.1	44.8
1952	+38.7	+54.5	50.1	+8.0	46.0
1953	+34.6	+57.6	53.4	+4.2	50.4
	+166.2	+266.7	297.6	–27.3	272.3
1954	+16.4	+42.9	54.7	–11.9	52.4
1955	+1.8	+26.2	57.2	–30.6	53.8
1956	–16.5	+4.5	58.9	–54.7	54.7
1957	–27.1	–3.7	59.8	–70.1	61.9
1958	–48.1	–28.1	60.9	–104.8	72.4
1959	–40.3	–12.59	61.2	–99.5	82.8
1960	–67.7	–47.8	64.6	–133.4	92.7
1961	–86.9	–53.4	68.6	–160.2	102.8
1962	–104.0	–69.2	74.4	–182.6	101.7

Source: *Annual Report and Accounts,* British Transport Commission, 1948-62.
From 1957 allocation does not include interest on accumulated railway losses and
on new borrowing. Both these items were transferred to a special account.

The Transport Act, 1953, marked a major step in the direction
of the complete disintegration of the British transport system.
The largely uncontrolled development of road haulage which
followed its passing ate into the revenue of the railways and
thence undermined the finances of the BTC. The Act was
responsible for creating many of the transport problems of the
second half of the twentieth century. With British Railways
deficits mounting, passenger fares were raised and the relative

attractiveness of private motoring increased. The number of passenger vehicles on the roads grew from 2½ million private cars and 962,000 motor cycles in 1952 – the year before the Transport Act was passed – to 12¾ million private cars and 1,082,000 motor cycles twenty years later. For most of the second half of the century ministers saw the problem as a railway problem rather than as a transport: road, rail, canals, coastal shipping and air services problem. This blinkered approach will be examined in the next chapter.

Chapter Nine: Notes

1. B. Donoghue and G.W. Jones, Herbert Morrison: Portrait of a Politician, (1973); John D. Mackintosh, 'Morrison, Herbert Stanley', in Dictionary of National Biography, 1961-70, (ed. F.T. Williams and C.S. Nicholls), (1981), pp.769-773.
2. Labour Party Annual Conference, Report, (1932), pp.211-14.
3. Trades Union Congress, Annual Report, (1933), pp.370-74.
4. T.R. Gourvish, British Railways, 1948-73, (1986), p.17.
5. Ibid., p.18.
6. The Times, 24 October 1943.
7. T.R. Gourvish, Ibid., pp.21-3.
8. F.W.S. Craig, British General Election Manifestos, 1990-1974, (1975).
9. Commons, Hansard 5th ser. vol.416, 19 November 1945, cols.34-36.
10. W. Plowden, The Motor Car and Politics, 1896-1970, (1971), p.84.
11. S.E. Finer, Anonymous Empire, (rev.edn. 1966), pp.93-4.
12. Ernest Davies, National Enterprise, (1946), pp.160-1.
13. R.M. Martin, TUC Growth of a Pressure Group, 1868-1971, (1980), p.290.
14. T.R. Gourvish, op.cit. pp.25-6.
15. Ibid, p.5; D. Henshaw, The Great Railway Conspiracy, (1991), p.44.
16. Commons, Hansard, 5th ser. vol.431, 17 December 1946, cols.1808-9.
17. Frederic Smith, 'The Future of Transport' in Labour Research, (March-April 1947), pp.49-50.
18. Cited in W. Plowden, p.85.
19. Box file of BRF publications, British Library reference WP/1784.
20. BRF, Annual Report, 1946-7, p.5.
21. BRF, Annual Report, 1945-6, p.5, and Annual Report 1946-7, p.6,

for the Minister's response to a deputation on 30 July 1946.

22. British Road Federation, Committee of Management, Annual Report, October-December 1947, p.11.

23. BRF, Annual Report, 1946-7, p.6.

24. Commons, Hansard, 5th ser. vol.507, speech of E. Davies 17.11.1952, col.1533.

25. T.R. Gourvish, op.cit. p.27.

26. Craig, op.cit.

27. Statement by Sir A. Lennox-Boyd in Commons Second Reading debate, 17 November 1952, Hansard, 5th ser. vol.507, col.1415.

28. PRO, Cab 128/24, 10 February 1952.

29. PRO, Cab 128/24, 7 and 30 October 1952.

30. Commons, Hansard, 5th ser. vol.507, cols.1624 and 1698-9, 18 November 1952.

31. Sir Gilmour Jenkins, The Ministry of Transport, (1959), p.114.

Chapter Ten
Railway Modernisation and the Beeching Plan

In the Commons' Second Reading debate on the Transport Bill of 1952 Sir Ralph Glyn, the Conservative MP for Abington, warned both his colleagues on the government benches and their Labour and Liberal opponents that they were

> talking too much about roads and about railways instead of about Transport with a big T .... if speakers in this debate keep on dividing the question into rail and road, we shall not give the impression of joint working which is so important.[1]

A study of Parliament's reaction to transport developments in the next three decades suggests that this warning went largely unheeded.

Following the enactment of the Transport Bill in 1953 it was inevitable that the finances of the British Transport Commission would be adversely affected by the, largely unrestricted, growth of road freight transport and especially by the rocketing number of 'C' licence vehicles on the roads. The abolition of petrol rationing just before the Transport Bill was passed, and the expansion of manufacture and sale of motor vehicles ensured that the growth of road passenger transport would also eat into the revenues of the BTC. Furthermore, the influence of the road lobby on public opinion and government policy was growing. As an example that Parliament was still thinking of 'road' and 'rail' separately, the Commons' debate of 28 May 1954, initiated by Mr Harmer Nicholls, MP for Peterborough, a supporter of the road lobby, may be cited. He moved the resolution:

> That this House, whilst it appreciates the Government's action in trebling the expenditure on major road improvements and development compared with past years, further urges, in the interest of road safety and industrial efficiency that an even more extensive road programme is inaugurated.

The speakers who followed the proposer of the motion gave illustrations of the inadequacy of the roads in their constituencies. Not one of them made reference to any other form of transport except motor vehicles and the adequacy or inadequacy of the road network to accommodate them.[2]

Before the bulk of the Road Haulage Executive's assets had been sold off under the Transport Act of 1953 the profits earned by British Road Services – the organisation of the publicly owned road freight transport industry – were healthy and showing signs of rapid expansion, as Table 2 on page 89 shows. Between 1951-3 inclusive the BTC was in surplus, even after meeting all the (unrealistically high) central charges, as Table 4 on p.91 reveals. After the mid fifties the earnings of both BRS and British Railways freight traffic declined sharply, bringing crisis to the finances of the BTC whose deficit, after payment of central charges, soared from £30.6 million in 1955 to £104.8 million in 1958. It was a crisis affecting the whole of British Transport, but successive governments treated it simply as a crisis in railway organisation and finance.

Aggravating the situation, as Mr Enoch Powell pointed out in the Commons on 3 February 1955, was the fact that the BTC had to pay a fixed interest on all its British transport stock irrespective of whether the economy was flourishing or in the doldrums. The privately owned railway companies before 1948 were capitalised through a variety of securities. The debenture stock had a prior claim on their earnings and paid a fixed rate of interest, but dividends paid on ordinary shares varied with the level of railway business. They acted as a buffer against trade depression.

Before it was disbanded and its work transferred to the British Railways Board or Area boards under the Transport Act, 1953, the Railway Executive was fully aware of the necessity to improve the efficiency of train services and therefore of the overriding need for investment in up-to-date equipment. A small committee of its members presented a confidential memorandum entitled Development Programme for British Railways, to the parent body in April 1953. When the BTC published its Modernisation and Re-equipment of British Railways – generally known as the Railway Modernisation Plan – in January 1955 it was similar in most of its proposals to the RE's Development

Programme except that the latter laid claim to £500 million of investment over 15 years while the later proposal of the BTC was estimated to need £1,250 million over the same period of time and the RE's plan had laid more emphasis on electrification of haulage while the BTC stressed the quick rate of return which could be expected from dieselisation.[3]

The Cabinet discussed the Modernisation Plan on 13 January 1955 and a week later. On both occasions differences of view were expressed. The pro-road ministers urged that the government should proceed with caution since 'in years to come roads, and perhaps aircraft, would take over much of the traffic now carried by the railways'. Those who supported the BTC's proposals pointed out that in the next 15 years £600 million would in any case be needed to maintain the system in its present state. The £400 million earmarked for the current road programme should be compared with the £210 million set aside for rail track modernisation under the Plan and not with the £1,250 million, £630 million of which was to be spent on new locomotives and rolling stock. R.A. Butler, the Chancellor of the Exchequer, reassured doubters by pointing out that the capital investment envisaged would be provided to the extent of £400 million from the BTC's own revenues while the remaining £800 million would be raised on government guarantee from the capital market. On balance, therefore, the Cabinet considered the Modernisation Plan should be adopted.[4]

The settlement of a long-standing dispute about railway workers' wages came just before the publication of the Modernisation Plan. A Court of Enquiry into the question presented an Interim Report on 5 January 1955 which found, that

> railwaymen should receive a fair and adequate wage
> and that, in broad terms, the railwayman should be
> in no worse case than his colleagues in comparable
> industry.[5]

With the acceptance of this Report by both government and rail workers' unions, the strike threat was removed. Harold Watkinson, Parliamentary Secretary to the Minister of Labour, to whom the Cabinet gave the job of commending the Modernisation Plan to Parliament, said that it was now assured that the unions would back it and that the improvements it would bring to railway efficiency would provide the means to give railway workers a fair wage. In a statement of naive optimism he declared:

> We believe that the railway industry has it within its own power to get out of deficit and into profitable operation and that it can do so by its own efforts. In other words, we want the nationalised industry to pay its own way without outside help.[6]

Later in the debate R.A. Butler endorsed the comments of his colleague by asserting that 'solvency must be assured by modernising plant and equipment'.

> 'In our view', he continued, 'there will clearly be competition for both passengers and goods between railways and roads. This is as it should be'.[7]

This approach was challenged by Herbert Morrison from the front opposition benches, who said:

> It is not enough that each element in transport shall do its duty by the public. It is vitally important that the various elements of transport shall co-operate so that we shall have a collective transport system in which the public is being served.[8]

What was notable was that the government did not scale down the level of BTC's debts or cancel the debts altogether. It simply eased the conditions of repayment. By contrast, the £71 million debt incurred by the private railway companies, after the winding-up of the wartime Railway Executive Committee and until the Transport Act of 1947 came into operation on the following 1st January, was wiped out and the Bill footed by the taxpayer.[9]

Far from ushering-in a turnaround of the railways finances, the early implementation of the Modernisation Plan brought for the first time an *operational*, as distinct from financial (i.e. the result after payment of central charges), deficit. It was £16½ million for the year 1956.[10] By 1958 BR's operational deficit had risen to £48 million compared with £27 million in the previous year. The BTC's other services including buses, London Transport, ships, docks and inland waterways earned a working surplus of £20 million; but this did not prevent the Commission's finances as a whole plunging deeper into the red.[11] A business recession in 1958 adversely affected railway freight revenues and resulted in the Board's deficit for that year rising to £90.1 million. Alarmed at this depressing news, the government looked again at the state of progress of the Modernisation Plan and in July 1959 published its White Paper Reappraisal of the Plan for the Modernisation and Re-equipment of British Railways. It re-valued the cost of the Plan to £1,500,000; provided some relief of the railways' burden of interest payments and expressed the hope that with continuing modernisation and easier short-term financial commitment the freight revenue of the railways would return to 1957 levels by 1963. Unfortunately, by that year they were 20 per cent below the 1957 levels.[12]

Part of the cost of the railways' deteriorating finances was paid by the railway work force whose wages fell below those earned by staff in comparable industries. Faced with the threat of a strike, the government of Harold MacMillan, in November 1958, set up a committee chaired by C.W. Guillebaud to examine the relativity of pay of BR staff with the pay of staff in other nationalised industries. The committee's report, published on 4 March 1960, recommended wage increases ranging from 8 to 18 per cent for the different grades of railway staff. It was clear that the implementation of the committee's findings would drive the Railway Board's finances further into the red unless some kind of structural reforms of the BTC were carried out.

Speaking in the Commons on 11 March 1960, Harold MacMillan accepted that 'fair and reasonable wages' must be paid to railway workers, but there were two important consequences. 'The public would have to accept the need for change in the size and structure of the industry' and 'there would have to be a radical alteration in the structure of the BTC, so that with a decentralisation of management, individual undertakings, including the regions of BR ... would be fully self-accountable'.[13] In a statement made the same day, MacMillan referred to 'an ever-increasing use of all forms of road transport' as the principal cause of the crisis in the BTC's finances.[14]

To make recommendations for applying the general principles outlined by the Prime Minister in his speech of 11 March the Cabinet appointed a committee under the chairmanship of Sir Ivan Stedeford. Its members had the advantage of the Minutes of Proceedings and Report of the Select Committee on Nationalised Industries: British Railways (1960) being available to them. That report had made clear that it would be no solution to the railways' financial problem to attempt to raise fares and freight charges. The general public was under the illusion that since 1938 fares had risen more steeply than the general cost of living. This was not so. Over that span of time fares had risen by 145 per cent, but general prices had gone up by 171 per cent. The Select Committee was in no doubt, however, that 'a rise in fares drives people away from the railways'. Motorists' immediate or perceived costs were often lower than the costs of rail travel, though the costs to the nation of motorised transport could be higher. Stedeford therefore offered a completely new structure of transport under the direction of the Minister who endorsed the committee's recommendations which in turn were adopted by the Cabinet.[15]

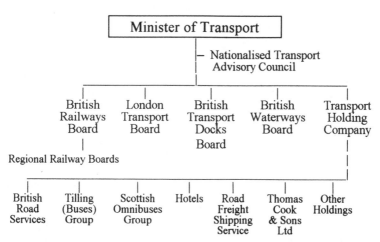

Source: Reorganisation of the Nationalised Transport
Undertakings, Cmnd 1248, December 1960.

The government's case was that the activities of the BTC were 'so large and so diverse' that it was 'virtually impossible to run them effectively as a single undertaking' and that its commercial operations were hampered by outmoded statutory obligations'. Separate Boards of Management for each of the then undertakings of the BTC would ensure clearly defined tasks which would guarantee more efficient operation. The Nationalised Transport Advisory Council had the responsibility of advising the Minister on the co-ordination of the work of the various Boards.[16]

The government's proposals were embodied in the Transport Act, 1962, under which the BTC was abolished and its diverse undertaking transferred to the various boards the White Paper of 1960 had envisaged. These were given far more commercial freedom than had been enjoyed by the Commission.

How far were the expectations of Ernest Marples, the Minister of Transport, fulfilled in the months and years ahead? The British Railways Board overall deficit which was £135.6 million in 1963 fell to £123.3 million in 1964, but then rose steadily to £153 million in 1967, despite more favourable interest payment terms under the 1962 Transport Act. The reorganisation of the various transport undertakings had clearly not improved the financial position of the railways.

When the British Railways Board assumed responsibility for running the railways of the country from 1 January 1963 the man chosen to be its chairman was Dr Richard Beeching (later Lord Beeching) who had gained a very high reputation as Chairman of Imperial Chemical Industries and since 1 January 1961 had been Chairman of the BTC.

In the autumn of 1962 the Cabinet of Harold MacMillan was far more concerned with Dr Beeching's proposals for settling the claims of the railway workers than it was with the rail closure plans which were taking shape. Dr Beeching was both concerned to maintain his reputation as a good employer which he had gained as Chairman of ICI, and keen to forestall any opposition the railway unions might have to his plans for their industry. He therefore informed Ernest Marples, the Secretary of State for Transport, that he would be prepared to offer the unions a rise of 6 per cent with a possibility of increasing it to 7 per cent after discussions. The Cabinet, which was thinking of a 3 per cent norm for workers in the nationalised industries, was alarmed, and its meeting on 29 October 1962 decided to instruct Richard Maudling, the Chancellor of the Exchequer, to write him a private letter, 'not intended for publication', informing him that 'a figure of 6 per cent was unacceptable to the government'.[17] The deadlock was overcome when the cabinet decided at its meeting on 1 November 1962 to make a lump sum of £16 million available to the Chairman for settling the railway workers' claims.[18] It was not until 14 March 1963 that the Cabinet received a report from its Committee on the Reorganisation of Railways advocating the endorsement of Dr Beeching's Plan, though it would involve 'drastic alterations in the existing system, and substantial curtailment of services, especially in the more remote parts of the country'.[19]

The Beeching Report – The Reshaping of British Railways – was published on 27 March 1963 and included the closure of approximately one third of the route mileage and no less than 2000 railway stations. The majority of the 29 railway workshops then in business would also be closed and the manufacture and maintenance of locomotives and rolling stock concentrated on a few of the best equipped shops such as those at York and Derby. Freight traffic would be concentrated through 100 depots, and emphasis would be given to the development of the liner train services for the movement of freight. Although staff numbers had been reduced by 26.9 per cent since 1948, there would inevitably be further staff losses. Those made redundant would be given a lump sum equal to two-thirds of their weekly wage multiplied by the number of years they had been in service.[20]

In commending the Beeching Report to the Commons, Ernest Marples presented an alarming picture of what would happen to the future finances of the railways. In 1963 the deficit would be £150 million but then, 'about 1970, it would be astronomical'. The country 'could not afford to delay the implementation of the Plan'. He did not claim that there would be any wonderful transformation of the situation through its adoption: 'if the railways attract all the freight which they want from the roads, this will reduce road traffic by 2 per cent'.[21] In reply, Harold Wilson, the Leader of the Opposition, warned that

> To close one sector of the railway system affects all the others, because traffic arising in one area affects the profitability of the rest of the system. All parts of the system are members one of another, so when one closes part of this it is not an ordinary business transaction. It is more in the nature of an amputation.

The government had followed a judicial procedure made familiar in Alice in Wonderland – sentence first, verdict afterwards. It was 'totally wrong to base a decision on a narrow obsession with railway accountancy'.[22] Wilson's colleague John Hynd, in a very perceptive speech, stressed that the Beeching Plan would not bring the hoped-for relief to the railways' fortunes. Quoting from a leading article of The Times he pointed out that

> the comparative prices of road and rail transport bear little relation to their true comparative costs. . . . The railway accounts would look very different if the costs of sustaining the network were no more than the amounts spent annually on new permanent way. A road fund licence buys unlimited access to a nationwide road system built up over the years, with no charge for accumulated capital and interest nor for a wide and costly range of ancillary services. Road charges bear little relation to cost. . . . By an adjustment of the taxation item alone, the government could solve the railway problem and get traffic from road to rail.[23]

In the General Election of 15 October 1964 the Labour Party, under the leadership of Harold Wilson, secured a majority of 4 seats over the Conservatives and Liberals together and on the following day formed a new government. Richard Beeching was still Chairman of British Railways. Labour Party supporters, who hoped for a radical change from the Marples policies after the election victory, were disappointed when they learned that the new Transport Minister was to be Mr Tom Fraser, a charming man, but not a forceful and positive character. His appointment was an indication that Harold Wilson was not giving priority to new directions in transport policy. At the second meeting of the new Cabinet he (Tom Fraser) said that he had no immediate intention of reversing the closure policies of his predecessor. It was George Brown, the First Secretary of State, who made the proposal at the second meeting of the Cabinet on 15 December 1964 that Dr Beeching, who was due to retire as Chairman of the British Railways Board at the end of that month, should stay on to make 'a study of transport co-ordination on the understanding that he would devote his whole time to this undertaking before returning to private industry on 1 June 1965'. Tom Fraser said that his ministry was committed to prepare a national plan for the co-ordination of transport and that he would welcome the proposal. Some ministers expressed reservations because the trade unions would be against the proposal, since the Beeching Plan of March 1963 involved the loss of thousands of railway jobs, and that Dr Beeching might well be tempted to act in an executive capacity as a kind of 'Overlord' of transport. To overcome these doubts it was decided that he

> should be assisted by a strong panel, comprising rep-
> resentatives of the road and rail trade unions, the road
> haulage interests, and independent individuals with
> experience of the economics of transport. It would be
> preferable that the members of the panel should not be
> regarded as merely assessors but that they should take
> an active part in the enquiries and discussions leading
> to the final report.[24]

Why did the Wilson Cabinet think it wise to invite Dr Beeching to stay on to study transport co-ordination? It considered that although he had cut rail services drastically, he had – by the standards of the time – treated fairly generously staff who were victims of the changes. Moreover, if he looked into the situation of road freight haulage he might discover, as John Hynd had done, that the prices of road and rail freight transport bore little relation to their true comparative cost[25] and might recommend changes in the taxation of road freight vehicles which would then place railways in a better competitive position. It was not to be. Beeching turned down the invitation and returned to ICI because he did not like 'the strings attached to the job at the Ministry of Transport – the 'advisory committee alongside which he would have had to work.[26]

Since 1953 governments had advanced three major schemes to reverse the decline in the relative part played by railways in the total of British transport services and to counter their rapidly growing deficits. These were the Railway Modernisation Plan of 1955, the abolition of the BTC and the structural reorganisation of services under the Transport Act of 1962 and the Beeching Plan of 1965. They all failed.

Why was this the case? There are two main aspects of the answer. Firstly, in each case the railways were treated in isolation from the other forms of transport, and this was in face of the fact that each form of transport has an impact on other modes, as they do on it. Secondly, motorised transport, but especially freight vehicles, did not pay the full cost of the roads they used.

In his speech of 29 April 1963 Ernest Marples, aware of the criticism from the opposition that the Beeching approach was too one-sided, proposed

> to re-examine the fundamental basis and working of the road licensing system for road goods transport. An independent committee of enquiry was therefore to be appointed to examine the whole question of licensing road haulage and to make recommendations.[27]

Lord Geddes[28] was shortly afterwards appointed chairman of this committee.

The BRB gave the most detailed evidence to the committee in its submission entitled <u>A Study of the Relative Cost of Road and Rail Freight Transport</u>. It claimed that each form of transport should pay its fair share of track costs and this was not currently happening:

> Comparing a 4 track trunk rail route, a 2 lane dual carriageway trunk road and a 3 lane dual motorway, the cost per capacity ton–mile (including the cost of buying land, providing new track, maintenance and providing ancillary services, such as signalling, policing and lighting) (but excluding terminal costs) was 0.37 d for a ten ton covered railway van, 0.81 d for

a ten ton vehicle on a trunk road, and 0.70 d for a similar vehicle on a motorway. Comparable costs for a 12½ ton liner train container and a 16 ton road vehicle were 0.34 d and 0.76 d (trunk road) and 0.65 d (motorway).

If a road haulage operator was prepared to bear his full share of the true cost of the motorways and trunk roads which he used, his contribution would rise from about £1,400 (representing the licence duty and fuel tax) to about £3,500. Such a change would materially increase the margin which rail enjoyed over all but the shortest of distances.[29]

At a press conference on 23 June 1964 Dr Beeching said that the report offered an alternative to nationalisation as a means of achieving a balance between road and rail.[30]

It was not until a year later that the Geddes Report Carriers' Licensing, appeared. It was influenced by very strong and well-financed written evidence from the British Road Federation, the Road Haulage Association, the Society of Motor Manufacturers and Traders and the Ministry of Transport itself, which was heavily dominated in personnel and resources by road, rather than rail, transport.[31] The members of the Geddes Committee could not see how there could be a switch from road to rail freight 'without an administrative machine of inordinate size; of doubtful efficiency and without placing a heavy burden on industry and trade'. Taxation was 'an obvious tool, but one which was difficult to use precisely in practice'.[32] However, earlier in the Report the admission was made: 'We did not enquire into these aspects.'

Rather than having exaggerated the true costs of road freight transport, the BRB had underestimated them. At that time there were no accurate and reliable figures for the cost of road accidents for which lorries were partly responsible. The costs of congestion in the form of lost working hours were not included. Even if the BRB report was partly true, the increase in lorry taxation so that it more nearly reflected true costs of road freight operation would have persuaded some consignors of goods to switch to rail freight.

Chapter Ten: **Notes**

1. Commons, Hansard, 5th ser. vol.507, 17 November 1952, col.1508.
2. Commons, Hansard, 5th ser. vol.528, 28 May 1954, cols.769-789.
3. T.R. Gourvish, British Railways, 1948-73, (1986), pp.257-64.
4. PRO Cab 128/37, 13 January 1955.
5. Commons, Hansard, 5th ser. vol.536, 3 February 1955, col.1327.
6. Ibid., col.1282.
7. Ibid., col.1303.
8. Ibid., col.1320.
9. See E. Popplewell's Commons speech, Hansard, 5th ser. vol.507, 17 November 1952m col.1489.
10. BTC Annual Report for 1956, published on 28 June 1957.
11. BTC Annual Report for 1958, published on 24 June 1959.
12. T.R. Gourvish, op.cit. p.296.
13. Commons, Hansard, 5th ser. vol.619, cols.642-44.
14. The Times, 12 March 1960.
15. PRO, Cab 128/34, 1 and 9 December 1960.
16. Reorganisation of the Nationalised Transport Undertakings, Cmnd 1248, December 1960, §§ 9-11, p.4.
17. PRO Cab 128/36, 29 October 1962.
18. Ibid., 1 November 1962.
19. Ibid., 14 March 1963.
20. Ernest Marples, Commons Hansard, 5th ser. vol.676, col.726, 29 April 1963.
21. Ibid., col.722 et.seq.
22. Ibid., cols.908-16.
23. Ibid., cols.768-75.
24. PRO Cab 128/39, 15 December 1964.
25. Commons, Hansard, 5th ser. vol.676, col.726, 29 April 1963.
26. T.R. Gourvish, op.cit. p.344.
27. Commons, Hansard, 5th ser. vol.676, col.739, 29 April 1963.
28. Formerly Sir A.C. Geddes, brother of Sir Eric Geddes, First Secretary of State for Transport.
29. BRB Estimate of the true comparative costs of Providing Rail and and Road Freight Services, (June 1964). British Library reference number BS 122/75.
30. The Times, 24 June 1964.
31. Ministry of Transport, Carriers Licensing, (1965), Appendix A, List of Bodies and Persons who submitted evidence to the Committee.
32. Ibid., § 9.51 p.76.
33. Ibid., § 9.39 p.74.

Chapter Eleven
Barbara Castle's
massive Transport Act, 1968

After Labour's General Election victory of 15 October 1964 the new Prime Minister, Harold Wilson, was keen to give cabinet office to Barbara Castle who had campaigned with him in the run up to the election. She was offered, and accepted, the Ministry of Overseas Development and proved her ministerial capabilities in that office. On 23 December 1965 she was transferred to the Ministry of Transport as Secretary of State.

The Ministry she inherited was described by her as 'a huge sprawling jungle' of 7,000 civil servants patently in need of departmental reform.[1] There were 12 Under-Secretaries and 14 main departments. The overwhelming majority of the staff was concerned with road transport. The road lobby was, in fact, dominant. Nearly eight years later she told the House of Commons:

> When I took over as Minister of Transport the most vociferous lobby in the country was represented by road interests. The propaganda and pressure groups led by the British Road Federation said that we must concentrate all our resources on building the first thousand miles of motorway. The environment lobby had barely been born and when I tried to suggest that there were other considerations that we should bear in mind I had an uphill task.[2]

Barbara Castle's predecessor, Ernest Marples, had appointed Beeching 'to give effect to government intentions for its largest lossmaker to redirect resources into road transport'.[3] When she took office it was apparent that the Beeching Plan had failed to secure the balancing of the British Railways Board books. Sir Stanley Raymond, the Chairman, in his Annual Report and Accounts for 1965, described it as 'a difficult year'. Economies in working expenses 'were harder to obtain than in previous years, savings from the more obvious and easier sources having already been secured'. In a warning to government the Chairman wrote:

The railways can never be wholly viable without further action to relieve them of social burdens which, if they must be met, should be financed by sources other than railway revenues.[4]

That year the BRB had incurred a loss, after payment of interest, of £132.4 million. In the following year it was even larger, at £134.7 million.[5] In his Annual Report of 1966 Raymond expressed concern that, until the projected Transport Bill became law, implementing the governments decision to abandon the 1962 Transport Act's principle of commercial accountability, the Board would have to continue to support uneconomic services.[6]

Clearly all these problems had to be tackled and the Minister felt strongly that she 'had to build a transport policy from scratch'.[7] She began by building up a research and planning team, the Directorate of Economic Policy, whose chairman was Christopher D. Foster, an Oxford Economics don of 35 who was helped by Professor Michael Beesley of the London School of Economics. Their output, supervised by the Minister, comprised a series of Government White Papers on Transport Policy, Cmnd 3057 (July 1966); British Waterways, Cmnd 3401 (Sept. 1967); Railway Policy, Cmnd 3409 (November 1967); The Transport of Freight, Cmnd 3470 (November 1967); Public Transport and Traffic, Cmnd 3481 (December 1967); and Transport in London, Cmnd 3686 (July 1968). The first five of these publications included outlines of the main policies the Minister intended to incorporate in her Transport Bill. It was recognised that the proposals for London required separate legislation.

There was a strong body of opinion within the Labour Party that the Wilson government should restore the 1947 Transport Act in its entirety, including the re-nationalisation of all road haulage. Barbara Castle regarded this attitude as 'out of date' because there had been 'a dramatic switch of passenger and freight traffic from rail to road'. She was opposed to any attempt to restore the British Transport Commission. Following an interview with Lord Hurcomb, the first chairman of the Commission, she was persuaded that although the five executives under the BTC were supposed to be directed towards an integrated transport policy they were, in fact, left 'to go their own sweet way'.[8] She was determined to set up a new organisation, closer to the roots of business and transport to tackle the problem of transport coordination.

The Transport Bill, which Barbara Castle herself described as 'massive',[9] could have been split up into as many as 8 separate measures. It contained 169 Clauses and 18 Schedules. In its final form as the Transport Act, 1968, it extended to 280 pages.[10] Whilst admitting the Bill's length, the Minister claimed that there was through it all the unifying theme which she called 'practical socialism'. She shared Herbert Morrison's view that it was necessary to control all forms of transport, though she disagreed on the means by which transport coordination could be brought about. In a key sentence in her speech introducing the Transport Bill she said:

> Transport services must be planned in relation to each other – not allowed to go their own sweet way regardless of consequences.[11]

The first part of the Bill provided for the setting up of a National Freight Corporation with the aim of achieving 'properly integrated services by road and rail' and securing that goods were carried by rail wherever such carriage was 'efficient and economic'. With the consent of the Minister it could also organise transport movements by coastal shipping. In place of the Area Passenger Transport Boards Morrison had created under the Transport Act, 1947, Barbara Castle believed that in the Passenger Transport Authorities (PTAs) created under Part II of her legislation, she would achieve greater community participation in planning the bus and train services of their area, since the Authorities would be controlled by popularly elected local councils. Part III provided for the creation of a National Bus Company which would absorb the diverse bus services and companies previously under the umbrella of the Transport Holding Company, set up under the Transport Act, 1962. The Scottish Bus Group was also established as a separate organisation in 1968. The minister was empowered to give grants for bus services run by either of these concerns.

By 1966 the Board of British Railways had lost faith in the Beeching policy of cutting railway services as a means of restoring financial viability. It was pressing the Minister to accept the idea of government grants to support the non-commercial parts of the railway for 'social' reasons.[12] Barbara Castle incorporated plans for grants for 'unremunerative passenger services' in Part IV of her Act. These became known as the Public Service Obligation (PSO) grants and were part of the railway scenario until privatisation in 1994-6. The Minister was also convinced that a reasonable alternative to Beeching's root and branch policy of removing all tracks from closed lines was to remove those which were surplus to requirements, e.g. saving two out of four – whilst keeping open the railway routes. Under Part IV Section 40, therefore, provision was made for grant aid of up to £50 million, spread over five years, for the elimination of surplus track and signalling equipment.

In her autobiography Barbara Castle confessed she had 'always been fascinated by inland waterways'. She had spent some of her hours of relaxation on canal barges. After she took office as Secretary of State for Transport, therefore, she was

> horrified to discover that one of the Treasury's money-saving exercises in 1967 involved closing down miles of inland waterways which were no longer commercially viable.

But she persuaded Jack Diamond, of the Wilson government Treasury team, to give her 'enough subsidy to keep open 1,400 miles of non-commercially viable canals for pleasure cruising'.[13] Part VII of the Act gave effect to this concession. It divided the Waterways Board into two parts: one, known as the 'Commercial Waterways', mainly available for the carriage of freight, and the other, the 'Cruising Waterways', principally available for cruising, fishing and other recreational purposes. This was a commendable part of the Act from the point of view of amenity and the preservation of the environment, but it put paid to any plans for the expansion of long distance carriage of freight on British canals.

One of the most bitterly opposed parts of the Bill was Section 48 which gave powers to the Boards to manufacture goods for sale. Peter Walker of the Conservative opposition let it be known that 'he was spending £10,000 out of his own pocket' to employ a research team to help him 'kill the Bill'.[14]

The measures in Part V of the Bill were designed to exercise a greater control over the road freight vehicle operators. Section 60 made it illegal for any owner of a lorry or van to ply for hire or own use on the roads without a licence. Trips of over 100 miles by any road vehicle were classified as 'controlled journeys' which would not be allowed if BR or the PTAs could prove that alternative rail transport was available. The Transport and General Workers' Union welcomed the requirement (in Part VI) of a 10 hour limit of duty per day for freight vehicle drivers and of written records of a vehicle's movements. The recording instruments –spy in the cab– to prevent evasions of the law were also generally welcomed. The Act was notable for the introduction of breathalyser tests as a contribution to the reduction in the number of drunken driving cases. In the light of the fact that the Channel Tunnel was not opened until 1995, it is interesting to read under Section 143 that a Channel Tunnel Planning Committee was to be set up.

In the debate on the Bill, limited to one day, instead of the two which was customary for a major Bill, Peter Walker, the chief opposition spokesman, complained that it was 3½ times the length of the Steel Bill recently passed for nationalising the iron and steel industry. He stressed the adverse effect of the interference with road passenger and freight transport and prophesied that it was no solution for the financial troubles of BR.[15] From Barbara Castle's own back benches G.R. Strauss questioned the claim that through the PSO grants BR would become financially viable by the early 1970's. He said that he hoped that 'she would not pin her faith too closely on that expectation'. He noted that since the 1950's they had been told, at every major change in policy, that the railways would pay. But they never had.[16] His colleague, John Hynd, stressed the unequal burden of infrastructure costs as between road and rail. £179 million was loaded on to the railways in respect of tracks and signalling, for which there was no comparable burden on road transport.[17]

Considering that the Minister's expressed aim was to achieve the integration of all forms of transport her Bill had very little to say about coastal shipping. Since she was moved from Transport to Employment and Productivity in April 1968 it was left to Fred Mulley, her next-but-one successor, to introduce the Ports Bill in the Commons on 18 December 1969 with its objective of setting up a strong National Ports Authority. Its sponsors also hoped to improve industrial relations in the docks. Had it become law, it could have helped the Department of Transport to organise the move of more heavy freight to coastal tramps and liners. It passed both second and third readings in the Commons but had not passed the third reading in the Lords when Parliament was dissolved. The succeeding Conservative government under Edward Heath allowed the Bill to drop.

How far did the changes made in the 1968 Act help to improve the railways' position? Richard Marsh, who was appointed chairman of the BR Board on 9 September 1971, found that as a result of the Act's wiping out of BR's capital debts of £1,200 million and the new start that this dramatic intervention gave, the Board could claim that it made profits in 1969 and 1970. These were not sufficient for the Board to replace its assets, and a short time after he had arrived at the board it was 'sliding back into the red'.[18]

Figure 4 reveals how far Barbara Castle's optimistic expectation, that BR would become 'financially viable by the early 1970s', was wide of the mark and G.R. Strauss' doubts were justified. It shows that the organisation declared a net operating 'profit' in 1969 and 1970, as Richard Marsh had suggested; that in the next two years revenue was 'sliding back into the red' and that from 1973 to 1976 inclusive it was in the red. Figure 5 shows that the establishment of the National Freight Corporation did not result in any net switch of freight transport from road to rail though the growing importance of oil as an industrial fuel, rather than coal, gave some boost to coastal shipping (but a larger one to pipeline transport). At the time of the Transport Act, 1968, BR's share of the passenger market was just under 10 per cent. By the early eighties it had fallen to under 6 per cent. The railways' share of freight tonne mileage which was 19 per cent in 1968 fell to only 10 per cent in 1982.[19]

FIG. 4 British Rail: Net Railway Operations, profit or loss. £s million.

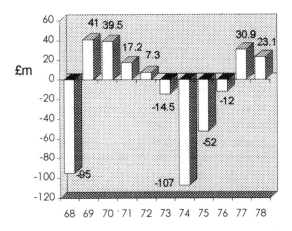

Source: British Railways Board, <u>Annual Reports and Accounts.</u>

Fig. 5 Freight Transport by mode 1968–1978 Goods lifted (million tonnes).

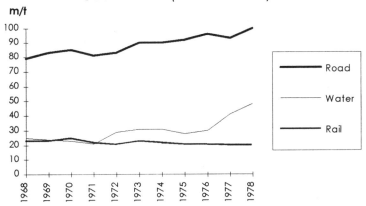

Source: Department of Transport;
<u>Transport Statistics Great Britain 1994 Edition</u>, p.181.

Barbara Castle and her dedicated team put in an immense amount of work to achieve their objective; so how was it that they had such a limited success ? The profitable part of BR's activities had been in the movement of freight. Their Act had set up <u>administrative</u> arrangements for the shifting of traffic from road to rail. What was lacking was a strong <u>fiscal</u> incentive to induce road freight operators to make the change. So long as it was cheaper for them to use the roads they would continue to do so. The increase in the number of heavier and longer lorries helped to frustrate the purposes of Part V of the 1968 Transport Act. The Society of Motor Manufacturers and Traders and the British Road Federation, through their influence in the Ministry of Transport, in 1955 managed to secure, unobtrusively, the raising of the maximum weight from 22 to 24 tons and were further successful in 1960 in raising the maximum weight again to 28 tons. It was being argued that the larger lorries were more economical to run and that deliveries to the supermarkets would be cheaper. So in 1964 the Ministry raised maximum weights yet again to 32 tons at the same time as it raised the speed limit from 30 to 40 mph and the maximum lorry length to 40 feet. Thereafter the road lobby met stiffer resistance from organisations such as the Pedestrian Association, the Civic Trust and, after 1972, Transport 2000. It took until 1981 for the government to opt for 40 ton lorries, though the road lobby had advocated a 44 ton limit.[20]

As permitted lorry weights increased and their number multiplied rapidly, the real cost of the fuel they used and the licence duty they paid, fell. They enjoyed an unfair advantage, especially on long distance trips, over other means of freight movement – the railways and coastal shipping. In 1980 there were 85,400 32-33 ton, four axle, articulated lorries, compared with only 41,500 in 1976. It was estimated that the 85,400 vehicles of 1980 received a £67 million subsidy (i.e. their fuel and licence duty taxes compared with the cost of the damage they did to the roads) and that the accumulated subsidy since fiscal year 1975-6 was £360 million.[21] <u>Figure 6</u> illustrates these points.

FIG. 6   National resource costs and tax revenue of
existing 32-ton articulated lorry. 1977/78.

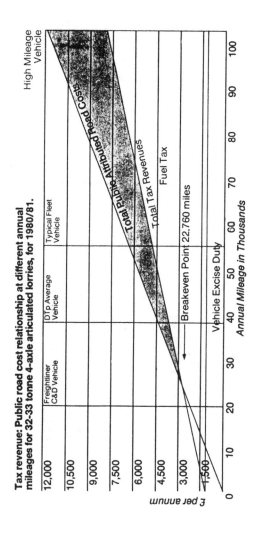

Sources: Dept of Transport
British Railways Board Facts and Figures 1980 p.23.

116

The favourable way of looking at BR's passenger traffic performance in the decade following the passing of the Transport Act, 1968, is to see that it stayed relatively steady at around 34-36 billion (thousand millions) kilometres annually. The more realistic way of viewing it is to recognise that private motorised passenger transport rose over the same decade from 292 billion to 390 billion kilometres, and that its share of all passenger transport rose from 75 per cent to 81 per cent. This upsurge in private car ownership and usage is explained partly by the fact that it became relatively cheaper to own and run a vehicle. Figure 7 shows that the taxes on car ownership (VAT + licence duty) fell from £69.27 in February 1960 to £50.68 in February 1980 at March 1980 money values. Figure 7 shows that the British public paid a lower rate of tax on petrol in 1980 than did people living in any of the other European Union countries except the Republic of Ireland. Figure 8 shows that in the UK taxes on car purchase and ownership were also falling.

FIG. 7 Taxes as a percentage of the purchase price of a gallon of petrol in November 1979

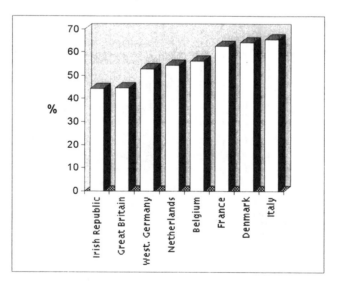

Source: Department of Energy
and British Railways Board Facts and Figures 1980

FIG. 8 UK Tax on Car Ownership (Excise duty + VAT)

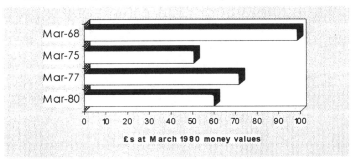

Source: British Railways Board Facts and Figures, 1980, p.23.

What angered Robert Adley, MP, the railway enthusiast, was that although all railway properties had been paying local taxes, (whether they were called rates or council tax) for over a hundred years, for a long time coaches and bus stopping points were not subject to local taxes. At Parliamentary question time on 15 November 1989, he asked the Local Government Minister, David Hunt, how much British Rail's rate Bill was for the financial year 1990-91 and he was told it was 'about £57½ million'. In his book the comment that immediately follows is 'Naturally, coaches ... will continue to park in the streets, paying nothing to do so, but creating congestion, wasting police time and polluting the air.'[22] The observations of a man of strong feelings, no doubt, but containing an element of widely accepted truth. It was largely the situation in Mr Adley's constituency of Christchurch.

A further reason for the bloated importance of private motor transport in the UK, and the failure of the legislation to redress the balance between rail and water transport on the one hand and road transport on the other, is the low esteem in which public transport has been held in British society and government. The name of the department was often changed after 1945 and aspiring cabinet ministers tended to regard the post as a stepping stone to 'better' things. Richard Marsh observed that when he took office as Secretary of State for Transport in April 1968, there had been 25 ministers in 50 years. In a number of cases they stayed less than a year in the post and it was common for the newcomer to have no specialist knowledge of transport matters. The politics of the business was basically short-term. There was no planning beyond the next General Election; and what national transport policy needed was someone with a long term vision at the helm. This was especially so in the light of the fact that the overwhelming majority of the staff in the Department were concerned with road transport. In France, by contrast, the health of public transport is regarded as a matter of national importance and state pride whether the President be a Mitterrand or a Chirac.

Chapter Eleven: **Notes**

1. T.R. Gourvish, British Railways, 1948-73, (1986), p.350.
2. House of Commons, Hansard, 5th ser. vol.859, 4 July 1973, col.556.
3. Robert Adley MP (Christchurch), Out of Steam: the Beeching Years in hindsight, (1990), p.12.
4. British Railways Board, Annual Report and Accounts, 1965.
5. T.R. Gourvish, op cit, Table 47, p.397
6. British Railways Board, Annual Report and Accounts, 1965.
7. Barbara Castle, The Castle Diaries, 1964-70, (1984), p.83.
8. Barbara Castle, Fighting all the Way, (1993), p.71.
9. Commons, Hansard, 5th ser. vol 756, 20 December 1967, col.1281.
10. Public General Acts, (1968), chapter 73.
11. Hansard, 20 December 1967, col.1282
12. T.R. Gourvish, op.cit., pp.351, 394.
13. Barbara Castle, Fighting all the Way, (1993), p.396.
14. Castle Diaries, 12 February 1948, p.372.
15. Hansard, 20 December 1967, cols.1304-7.
    See also, Richard Marsh, Off the Rails, (1978), pp.167-8.
16. Ibid., col.1322.
17. Ibid., col.1358.
18. Richard Marsh, interviewed by Robert Adley, Out of Steam, p.45.
19. T.R. Gourvish, op.cit., p.389.
20. Mick Hamer, Wheels Within Wheels, (1987), chap.7, pp.78-89.
21. Transport and Road Research Laboratory, report, LR 910, cited in British Railways Board, Facts and Figures, 2nd Edn. (1980), p.14.
22. Robert Adley, op.cit., p.37.

Chapter Twelve
Transport in the Thatcher years

In the General Election of 3 May 1979 the Conservatives gained over fifty seats from Labour and became the majority party. On 4 May Margaret Thatcher was at Buckingham Palace taking over the reins of office.

The new Prime Minister had a great respect for her father, a grocer in Grantham, and learnt from him the need to balance the business accounts, to pay debts promptly and to live within one's means. In her youth the motor car was a clear symbol of success and family and personal independence. In her maturity, as leader of the government party, she looked forward to the UK being 'a car-owning democracy'. One of her strongly held beliefs was that 'state owned businesses can never function as proper businesses'.[1] She shared the view of her mentor Sir Keith Joseph who believed that high state spending crowds out enterprise and threatens freedom! She travelled by train only on very rare occasions. The BBC Nine o'Clock News on Friday 6 February 1987 showed her travelling to Scarborough to the Conservative Party Conference on an InterCity train. She said "I must come this way again". But the previous time she had travelled by train was en route to Gatwick during the General Election campaign of 1983 and in the years after 1987 there was no evidence that she used this means of transport more frequently than she had done earlier.

The new leader's views on the respective merits of rail and road as means of transport were reflected in the government support for the railways through the Public Service Obligation (PSO) grant and the expenditure on road building. Figure 9 shows that in 1990, in real terms, the PSO was less than half the level of 1980. By contrast, Figure 10 shows that government expenditure on road construction and maintenance was in 1990 more than three times the level of expenditure of 1980. It is noteworthy that, in the terminology of the age, the government 'invested' money in the roads but 'subsidised' the railways.

120

FIG. 9 Public Service Obligation (PSO) Grants to British Railways by Thatcher governments, 1982-1991

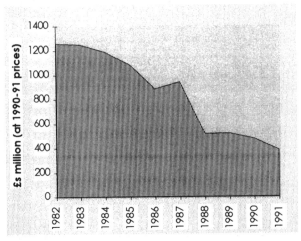

Source: Commons <u>Hansard</u>, vol.177, 26 July 1990, col.403. Written answer by Cecil Parkinson, Secretary of State for Transport, to question from Mr. Michael (Labour).

FIG. 10 UK Public Expenditure on Road Transport, 1981-90

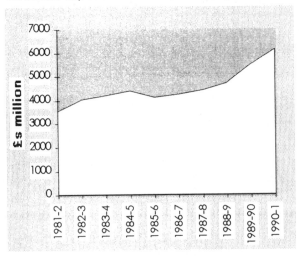

Source: <u>Transport Statistics Great Britain</u>, 1977-1987, Table 1.8 pp.33-4, and <u>Transport Statistics Great Britain</u>, 1994 Table 1.17 p.47.

Both, in fact, were paid for by the taxpayer, but the word
'investment' has a positive connotation, while contributions to
a subsidy were regarded as a burden, grudgingly given. In the
words of Charles Secrett:

> The criteria used for assessing a proposed road are
> different from those used for evaluating a new railway.
> Rail has to provide an economic return in cash terms
> after the costs of laying tracks, staffing and rolling
> stock are taken into account. Roads are not subject to
> the same restraints.[2]

Since it was the accepted government philosophy that high
state spending crowds out enterprise, strict limits were imposed
on the railways' borrowing powers through the External
Financing Limit (EFL). The reduction of both the PSO and the
EFL in real terms necessarily meant that BR was obliged largely
to restrict itself to essential maintenance and renewal and had
little to spare for new developments. John Wells, of the Faculty
of Economics in the University of Cambridge, pointed out that
as far back as the early 1960's railway investment was running
at almost twice the level of 1987.[3] Sir Bob Reid, the
Conservative who had been appointed by Margaret Thatcher as
Chairman of the British Railways Board, expressed the situation
in more homely terms when he wrote: 'When it comes to
funding, the railways have always been tail-end Charlie'.[4] The
leader writer of The Times was equally forthright:

> Foreign rail managers, fat with subsidy, visit Britain to
> wonder in amazement that its trains run at all. The rest
> of Europe puts five times as much into its railways as
> does Britain. ... In France a minister boasts of his new
> rail plans. In Britain a transport secretary wins his
> spurs by crushing them.[5]

The Conservative Party's election manifesto, published on
11 April 1979, was deceptively modest in its statement of objectives for British transport in the forthcoming session. It read:

> We aim to sell shares in the National Freight
> Corporation to the general public in order to achieve
> substantial private investment in it. We will also relax
> the Traffic Commission's licensing regulations to

enable new bus and other services to develop – particularly in rural areas – and we will encourage new private operations.

The Queen's speech to the new Parliament on 15 May was more generalised and vague in the promise 'to reduce the extent of nationalised and state ownership and increase competition'.

However, when Norman Fowler, the Minister of Transport, moved the second reading of the Transport Bill in the House of Commons on 27 November 1979 it was clear that the government envisaged far-reaching changes in public road transport services. The Bill, which became law as the Transport Act of 30 June 1980, abolished the need for licensing – except for roadworthiness – of coaches engaged in express services, i.e. those of thirty miles or more between stops, and of coaches engaged in excursion traffic. The second major part of the Act was to change the publicly owned National Freight Corporation to a private company with shares sold to the public. Albert Booth, the chief opposition spokesman on transport, stressed the damage which would be inflicted on the bus industry through the Bill's enactment;[6] but it may be argued that the greatest damage was done to BR's passenger services through the unleashing of the competition of express coaches with the railways InterCity services. Generally, except at main bus termini, such as Victoria Coach Station in London, express coaches at intermediate cities and towns on their route, could park free in the street. The companies concerned did not have to pay local rates (later, council taxes) as railway stations did. Not surprisingly they could undercut railway passenger fares, especially as there was less effective control over drivers' working conditions and pay than the NUR and ASLEF had over railway operating staff. The Transport Act, 1980, therefore played an important part in undermining the stability of the public transport industry in the UK.

Norman Fowler, the Secretary of State for Transport, who had recently been promoted to cabinet rank, introduced his second Transport Bill in the Commons on 13 January 1981, said that there were two main purposes to the proposed measure. The first was to introduce private capital into the subsidiaries of British Rail: British Transport Hotels; Sealink U.K.; British

Rail Hovercraft; the British Rail Property Board and the British Transport Docks Board. The second part of the Bill included provisions for road safety such as giving powers to local authorities to install road humps ('sleeping policemen') and a stiffening of the penalties for drunken driving.[7] The minister claimed that privatising the BR subsidiary concerns would free them from the Treasury restraints of the External Financing Limit (EFL) which curtailed their power to borrow for investment purposes. But Albert Booth, chief opposition spokesman on transport, declared that the Bill's principal purpose was to transfer mainly profitable organisations from the public to the private sector, depriving BR of an important source of revenue. There was no evidence that the proceeds of the sale would be added to the EFL and thus enable BR to make much needed investment; its main purpose was to reduce calls on the National Loans Fund.[8] Peter Snape MP stressed the urgent need for more investment, as the sums set aside for this purpose had been frozen at £305.5 million for several years and was even below the level of Belgium which spent £346 million on a much smaller network.[9]

An important consequence of the passing of the two Transport Acts of the early 'eighties and of the government's financial difficulties of those years was that the process of electrification of BR's network was greatly retarded. In its Annual Report and Accounts of 1982 the BR Board stated that

Electrification is the central issue for the railway future
– essential in practical terms, to achieve a more efficient,
attractive and thereby more profitable railway.

In February 1981 the BRB/Department of Transport Joint Review of Main Line Electrification recommended the major electrification option, covering services carrying up to 83 per cent of passenger traffic and up to 68 per cent of freight traffic. Norman Fowler rejected this proposal and declared, that only when InterCity lines reached commercial viability would the go-ahead for major electrification be given. This attitude hardened with the passing of time with the increasing influence of Mrs Thatcher's No10 'Think Tank', dominated by the monetarist Professor Alan Walters.[10] Although the case for a larger-scale programme of electrification was accepted by a wide cross-section of the community including the Commons all Party Transport Committee, the TUC and the CBI, only relatively small schemes were adopted including the Tonbridge/Hastings line approved in October 1983 and the Bishops Stortford/ Cambridge line given the go-ahead in the following January. The consequence was that by the end of the 1980's the UK had the lowest level (29%) of its railway track electrified of any country in Europe.[11]

The first Thatcher-dominated Parliament was dissolved on May 13, 1983, a year before the expiry of its full five year term. The Conservatives' General Election Manifesto gave priority to promises limiting the power of trade unions over privatisation in the transport sphere. However, there was a promise 'to introduce substantial private capital into the National Bus Company'. In the General Election of June 9 the Conservatives were returned with a greatly increased majority over all other parties. In the reorganisation of government which followed it is significant that Mr David Howell who had been Secretary of State for Transport and more to the left of the party, was not allocated any government post.

The Transport Bill which the Secretary of State, Nicholas Ridley, introduced to the Commons on 12 February 1985 proposed a far more comprehensive change in bus transport provision than the general election manifesto had suggested. The preamble to the Bill included the forthright statement that its object was

to make provision for the transfer of the operations of
the National Bus Company to the private sector.

In commending the second reading of the Bill to the Commons Ridley said, that 'its purpose was to halt the decline that [had] afflicted the bus industry for more than twenty years'. Competition was 'the key to increasing patronage' which would halt the decline and bring prosperity to the industry. One of the principal causes of the industry's decline had been 'the system of regulations and near monopoly – the fifty year old road service licensing rules'.[12] Thus section one of the Bill abolished road service licensing and it was claimed that henceforward –

according to the Secretary of State – 'operators would be free to provide the services that the customers want'.

Mrs Gwyneth Dunwoody, for the opposition, challenged the truth of Ridley's statements. She said, that in reality the Bill demonstrated that he had two obsessions which permeated its 138 sections and 189 pages. One was privatisation and the other deregulation. He had pushed ahead with the legislation irrespective of the fact that 'there was no proper evidence to prove that it was necessary'. A Select Committee of the House which had assembled much evidence on the state of the bus industry was due to publish its report in a few days' time; but he was not waiting for that.[13] The second obsession was his determination to reduce government expenditure on subsidies. Mrs Dunwoody's colleague, Gordon Oakes, was concerned that both services to the public and the working conditions of the drivers would deteriorate. Clause 81(3) of the Department of Transport's Explanatory Memorandum on the Bill, which dealt with tendering for subsidised bus services, read:

An invitation to tender under this section may not include conditions with respect to the terms of employment of persons to be employed in providing any service to which invitation to tender relates.[14]

In view of the government's large overall majority in the Commons the Bill's passage through Parliament was assured. It passed its second reading by 288 votes to 170 on 22 May. It became law on 30 October that year.

Subsequent government statistics reveal that the predictions made by Nicholas Ridley on the likely effect of the legislation on the future of the bus industry and enhanced passenger usage were unreliable. In Great Britain the number of passenger journeys by bus declined from 5,650 million in 1984 to 5,074 million in 1989-90. Thereafter they declined at an accelerating rate to 4,483 in 1992-3.[15] Bus journeys represented nine per cent of all journeys by road in 1984. They accounted for only six per cent of journeys in 1990.[16] Under the Transport Act, 1985, the fifty year old road service licensing rules about which Ridley had complained had been largely abolished, but following their abolition, the situation had got worse rather than better.

Far from 'competition being the key to increasing patronage' the opposite was the case. There was in many places a glut of buses in day-time rush hours but a scarcity, or disappearance, of all services in off-peak periods. With de-regulation came a decline in public transport revenue support from £364 million in 1984-5 to £212 million in 1989-90[17] and a consequent sharp rise in average fares between 1987 and 1989.[18] The National Loans Fund had certainly saved millions of pounds; but millions of carless citizens were left without bus services in off-peak periods.

The Thatcher years were prosperous ones for the motor industry. The number of private cars rose from 14 million in 1979 to twenty million in 1990 and the number of commercial vehicles rose from 1.6 million to 2.2 million over the same span of time. A Department of Transport estimate in 1979 was that companies purchased 49% of all cars sold, but the British Institute of Management claimed that the figure was as high as 70%.[19] There is no doubt that the UK leads the list of countries providing company cars. More than 96% of British company directors; 97% of heads of department; 96% of senior finance managers and 99% of marketing managers benefit from the 'perk' of a company car through the Treasury exempting these vehicles from the full rate of tax.[20] The market for company cars in the late 1970's absorbed 2.5% of Gross National Product (GNP).[21] Although, as we have shown above, the Public Service Obligation Grant (PSO) for the socially necessary railway fell from 0.4% of the GNP in 1978 to 0.1% in 1990.[22] The average household in Britain subsidised the company car owner to the extent of £300 a year. By contrast, it paid less than £50 in taxes to maintain essential parts of the railway system.

The attractiveness of the company car to its owner is that when it was undertaxed (until possibly the 1994 Budget) it provided cheap or free work journeys, offering little disincentive to long distance commuting; it released disposable income, enabling more expensive housing to be considered; out migration from the work place is more feasible.[23] Company cars are also very much an indication of status, and luxury car makers stress the additional comforts and driving aids they provide to the potential director, senior manager or other business executive. The advertisements boast of the speed which a model can reach from 0 to 60 or 70 m.p.h. Two full page adverts for one prestige car tempted the reader:

Run your fingers over the Californian Walnut. You will feel the cares of the office slip away, and you're not even out of the car park.[24]

The price of the car to those other than company car owners was £26,520. To those purchasers the cares they would have at the bank might well have outstripped any worries experienced at the office!

The consequences of the presence of two million company cars on Britain's roads had significance both to the transport situation and to social life. Their owners, with their families, lived a life apart from those whose circumstances obliged them to use public transport. They were less likely to appreciate the hardships caused by declining government support for train, bus and tram services. Their migration to the outer suburbs contributed to the congestion of the roads leading to inner city workplaces. Over half the daily journeys into and out of inner London are made in company cars.

In the later 1980's and in the 1990's Chancellors of the Exchequer began to accept the case for taxing some of the fiscal advantages that company car owners enjoyed. Incentives were given to employers to substitute cash allowances for the car 'perk'. In the Budget of March 1991 the Chancellor increased the scale charges for taxing employees on the value of the private use of company cars by 20 per cent.[25] In the Budget of March 1994 taxation was still further increased. These changes did not have the effects on the ownership of 'perk' cars that had been anticipated. A report in February 1996 noted that 'the perk car is as popular as ever' despite the fact an ever growing number of companies were offering cash allowances as a substitute.[26]

As is indicated in chapter two pp. 16-17, the Serpell Report of 20 January 1983 marked a decisive landmark in British railway policy. Sir Peter Parker welcomed the independent enquiry into BR's finances in the hope that it would accept the Board's case that it had been starved of funds for investment and that more government support for the railways would be recommended. Lord Marsh, former Secretary of State for Transport and BR Board Chairman, took a more hard-headed view. He wrote that 'fifty per cent of a so-called independent enquiry came from the very firms actually providing the advice and submitting the invoice at the end of it' and that 'the fees charged: £627,000, were outrageous in relation to any conceivable work which can have been involved'.[27] The Serpell Committee's terms of reference were that they were to examine the railway finances 'in the light of all relevant considerations'. But David Howell's letter to Sir David Serpell in September 1982 directed him to emphasise the reduction of railway operational costs. In consequence the Committee dismissed the case for higher investment in BR by claiming that the improvement that would be secured in operating results would not be sufficient to justify the increased investment.[28] On electrification the Committee commented that 'it did not consider the Board would be able to meet the conditions laid down by the government for approval of an electrification programme'.[29] They suggested that BR's safety standards might be unnecessarily high.[30] Replacing of signalling equipment was only justified 'when old equipment becomes so unreliable as to be unable to cater for the timetabled service'.[31]

In sum, the Serpell Report gave a clear indication that the Thatcher government's main concern about BR was to reduce its costs so that its books could be balanced as they had been at the Roberts' grocery store in Grantham.

Canals and Coastal shipping received little attention in the age of the market economy approach to transport. Goods carried within the British Isles fell by a third – from 9 million tonnes in 1983 to 6 million tonnes in 1993. Seagoing traffic on inland waterways fell from 2.1 billion tonnes in 1983 to 1.8 billion in 1993. The Coastal trade was also in a sad state of decline. Seagoing traffic at sea coastwise fell from 47.2 billion tonnes kilometres in 1983 to 37.5 billion tonnes kilometres in 1993.[32] Although the decline in the coastwise trade was mainly due to the reduction in coal and heavy metal shipments, the generally limited natural water courses in the UK and the uneconomic cost of short hauls plus the 'artificially' cheap cost of road haulage in heavy goods vehicles contributed to the shift of freight traffic from water to land. Canals and ports were not a government investment priority.[33] MPs representing ports were outnumbered by the members of the road lobby. Though there was a crying need for the diversion of heavy road freight to the environmentally friendly railways and inland and coastal waterways, the market economy approach to transport policy failed to secure this transference.

The Conservative Party's General Election Manifesto, The Next Moves Forward, of 19 May 1987 made three promises on transport matters.

> We are committed to a major capital investment programme through (1) New investment to build an extra 450 miles of motorway and trunk roads by 1989/90; (2) BR plans to invest £500 million a year over the next three years; (3) Private sector financing, construction and operation of the Dartford Bridge and the Channel Tunnel.

Robert Adley who was a Conservative member of Parliament for Christchurch throughout the years of Margaret Thatcher's premiership, sensed that, particularly after the 1987 election, there was among his colleagues a growing number of 'enemies of the railway'. These were made up of two elements, the 'roads lobby' and the 'anti-nationalisation fanatics'. He claimed that the members of the roads lobby were 'motivated by money, either as operators of road transport or as that industry's lobbyists', whereas the latter 'were mainly, but not exclusively, on the far right of the party, and believe quite simply that if its nationalised its useless'.[34]

It was these elements that in the closing years of Margaret Thatcher's third administration pressed hard for the complete privatisation of British Railways. BR's subsidiaries had been transferred to the private sector during her second parliament: now they pressed her to go for the jugular of BR itself. Their tactics were to ask loaded questions of the Secretary of State for Transport and of the Prime Minister herself. As a result of

Cabinet decision   and on the Premier's instructions in 1983
ministers informed questioners that, as Nicholas Ridley,
Secretary of State for Transport, said in reply to a question on
24 October 1983, that there were 'no grounds for believing that
we can privatise the railways in the near future'.[35] On 20 July
1989 Mr Goodlad asked Margaret Thatcher 'if she had received
recent representations regarding railway privatisation' and was
given the written answer that

> We are not yet ready to bring forward proposals for the
> privatisation of British Rail which would require
> careful preparation.[36]

However, during her last days at Number 10 she did think
seriously about the future of BR. In her memoirs she wrote:

> The other privatisation which I was considering was
> that of British Rail ... Cecil Parkinson and I considered
> how to proceed in October 1990. Cecil was keen to
> privatise the separate rail businesses – InterCity,
> Freight, Network South East. I, for my part, found
> attraction in the idea of a national track authority
> which would own all the track, signalling and stations,
> and then private companies would compete to run
> services. But these were large questions which would
> need careful thought and economic analysis. So I
> agreed with Cecil that a working party involving the
> Treasury and the DTI as well as the Transport
> Department be set up to study the issue and report
> back to me. That was as far as I could take the issue.[37]

The options for privatisation being considered in Downing
Street were the Omega Transport Policy of the Adam Smith
Institute which had advocated bus and rail deregulation ever
since 1984, and the Centre for Policy Studies advocacy of the
pre 1923 railway company structure. The form that the change
should take was the subject of disagreement. Both the Bob Reids
(Mark I 1985-90 and Mark II 1990-95) would have accepted
transference to the private sector, but only if the railways were
kept as an entity. Placing the infrastructure under a separate
authority, as had been done in Sweden, was not approved by
Malcolm Rifkind, who argued that it would bring many

problems as to the allocation of costs. Selling off the industry by sectors which was favoured by Cecil Parkinson would make the introduction of an integrated transport policy more difficult.[38] After the ousting of Margaret Thatcher as leader of the Conservative Party and her replacement by John Major there was less circumspection about transport policy in the leadership of the party and the stage was set for the introduction of the Transport Bill which became law in 1993.

On her assumption of office in the spring of 1979 Margaret Thatcher expressed her determination to inaugurate 'a radical change of direction' from a state-dominated to a free market economy. She confided in her memoirs that on becoming Prime Minister she shared the conviction which William Pitt, Earl of Chatham, expressed when he came to power in 1766: 'I know that I can save this country and that no one else can'. But did freeing Great Britain's transport from a large measure of state ownership serve the transport needs of the country well? Rather, it left a legacy of dependence on motorised transport with increasing problems of congestion and environmental pollution which the governments and people of the 1990's were under increasing necessity of resolving.

Chapter Twelve: **Notes**

1. M. Thatcher, The Downing Street years, (1993), p.677.
2. C. Secrett, The Environment: the government's record, (1992), p.46.
3. Letter to Financial Times, 16 December 1988.
4. The Observer, 17 February 1991.
5. The Times, 1 August 1990.
6. Commons, Hansard, 5th ser. vol.974, 27 November 1979, col.1133. See also J.S. Dodgson, Bus deregulation and privatisation, (1988), p.2.
7. Commons, Hansard, 5th ser. vol.996, 13 January 1981, col.855.
8. Ibid., col.864.
9. Ibid., col.903.
11. William Keegan, Mrs Thatcher's Economic Experiment, (1984), pp.156-7.
12. Charles Secrett, op.cit., p.47.
13. Commons, Hansard, 6th ser. vol.73, 12 February 1985, col.192.

132

14. Ibid., col.199.
15. Ibid., cols. 228-9.
16. HMSO, Transport Statistics Great Britain, (1994 edn.)
    Table 5.2, p.111.
17. Ibid., Table 1.1, p.35.
18. Ibid., Table 1.18, p.49.
19. Open University, New Towns Study Unit, Taxation of Company
    Cars, (1980).
20. Edinburgh Evening News, 14 March 1991, Financial Times,
    Recruitment and Personal Services supplement, 29 June 1988.
21. Motor Transport, 28 February 1977.
22. British Railways Board, Facts and Figures Section 7, International
    Comparisons 1978 and subsequent years.
23. Transport Studies Unit, Oxford University, Company Financing of
    Household Cars, typescript by M.C. Dix and R.R.T. Pollard (May
    1980).
24. Financial Times, 15 February 1991.
25. Financial Times, 20 March 1991.
26. Financial Times, 12 February 1996, Monks Guide to Company
    Car Policy, (1996).
27. Lords, Hansard, vol.439, No.56, col.1207, 2 March 1983.
28. Railway Finances, Report of a Committee chaired by Sir David
    Serpell, (1983), p.44.
29. Ibid., p.43.
30. Ibid., p.31.
31. Ibid., p.31. For further information on the Serpell Report see
    P.S. Bagwell, End of the Line? (1984), chapter 9.
32. HMSO, Transport Statistics Great Britain, (1994), Table 6.9,
    p.138.
33. D. Maltby and H.P. White, Transport in the United Kingdom,
    (1983), p.73.
34. Robert Adley, Out of Steam: the Beeching Years in hindsight,
    (1990), p.2.
35. Commons, Hansard, 6th ser. vol.47, 24 October 1983, col.45.
36. Commons, Hansard, 6th ser. vol.157, 20 July 1989, col.350.
37. Thatcher, op.cit., p.686.
38. Financial Times, 12 April 1989. Paul Salveson, British Rail: the
    radical alternative to privatisation. Centre for local economic
    strategies, Manchester (1989).

Chapter Thirteen
The Fight over the
Railways Bill, 1993

After John Major succeeded Margaret Thatcher as Prime Minister the parliamentary pressure of those described by Robert Adley as the 'anti-nationalisation fanatics' continued at an even more strident tempo. Sir John Stokes, the MP for Halesowen and Stourbridge, in a Commons Adjournment debate on 13 March 1991, painted a glamorous picture of the scene at Paddington in the 1930s and typified the approach of the extreme right wing:

> I remember the thrill of going to Paddington station en route to Oxford, and I remember the West Country accents, the chocolate and cream coaches, the glorious engines and, of course, the station master in top hat and tails. Apprentices for the GWR had to go to Swindon to be approved. It was like joining a good regiment. The Railways were privately owned and the morale of the staff was high.

By contrast, in 1991 there were 'frequent delays, the breakdown of engines and signalling, about which there was little or no information'. He was driven reluctantly to the conclusion that 'the weaknesses of management were due largely to security of tenure' and that 'the sooner all the separate services were privatised the better'.[1]

Roger Freeman, the Minister for Public Transport, replied sympathetically:

> My friend has suggested privatisation as the solution. The government would agree with him. ... The government have not reached any conclusion about the timing or the method of that – it is a very difficult task and one that must be done sensitively, with proper consultation and with proper forethought.[2]

There were undoubtedly differences about the method of privatisation, but by the end of January 1992 the most important of these had been hammered out. In the Conservative General Election Manifesto – <u>The Best Future for Britain</u> – of 5 February

1992, under the heading 'Transport' the promise was made that 'over the next three years there would be the biggest investment in Britain's transport infrastructure in our history', but there was no indication as to what proportion of this investment would go to roads and what to rail, though the specific promise was made that 'over the ensuing three years £6,300 million would be spent on trunk roads and motorways, concentrating on the bypass programme'. It was the intention 'to end BR's state monopoly' as this was 'the best way to produce profound and lasting improvements'. The private sector was to be given the opportunity to operate existing rail services and introduce new ones. In the light of subsequent developments it is significant that one part of BR was 'to continue to be responsible for all track and infrastructure' though its operating side would continue to provide passenger services only 'until they are franchised out to the private sector'. BR's freight operation would be sold outright. It was also proposed to sell off the more important stations as 'centres of activity'.[3]

For the same General Election the Labour Party Manifesto Time to get Britain working again promised to invest in decent public transport and 'to reject Conservative plans for privatisation of British Rail'. In place of bus deregulation, bus priority areas would be extended and new rapid transit systems, within a green light programme, would be designed to encourage travellers to switch from road to rail.[4]

A few weeks before the General Election of 9 April 1992 pollsters predicted a Labour victory. They were proved mistaken. The Conservatives, with 336 seats, emerged victorious with a lead of 21 over all the other parties.

In John Major's government John MacGregor, the Secretary of State for Transport, was aware that rail privatisation would be a difficult nut to crack compared with the earlier privatisation such as those of electricity and gas, where it was a case of taking over one or just a few organisations which were profitable going concerns, whereas most parts of BR were running at a loss. In cabinet therefore he urged that the initial steps towards rail privatisation should be taken in the first session of the new parliament if the necessary legislation was to be completed in its lifetime. Thus the intended legislative programme for railways was set out in the White Paper, New Opportunities for the Railways, published in July 1992. Although the authors of the paper conceded that BR's efficiency 'compared well with that of other European railways' and that the productivity of the BR workforce was 'among the highest of any European railway', passengers and freight customers were not getting the service they had a right to expect. The remedy lay in 'greater involvement of the private sector and the ending of BR's monopoly in the operation of services. It was conceded that 'it would not be practicable to privatise BR as a single entity' because its financial losses were too great. Privatisation on the basis of regional monopolies based on geography, or on business sectors, such as Trainload Freight, were both rejected. The key proposal, which provoked the greatest volume of questioning and opposition, read as follows:

> The government believes that track and train operations should be separated at an early stage and that a new track authority, Railtrack, should be established initially within BR, with responsibility only for track and associated infrastructure. When BR's train operations are in the private sector, Railtrack will continue on its own as a separate organisation.

In ministers' election propaganda and subsequently, the importance of bringing competition into the railway system had been constantly stressed. Thus, paragraph 15 of the White Paper read:

> The government proposes to provide a right of access to the rail network for private operators of freight and passenger services. All operators will be required to meet strict safety and environmental standards.

These proposals had of necessity to be dropped since it was also part of the government's plan for twenty five operating companies to run different parts of the railway service, and when it came to the point to inviting companies to bid for these franchises they were understandably loath to come forward if other concerns were to be given the right to run trains on the territory they had been allocated.

In the six months which elapsed between the publication of the White Paper and the Commons' Second Reading of the Railways Bill on 2 February 1993, transport ministers and officials of the Department of Transport were thinking on their feet as more details of the broad outline plans were filled in. There was also a storm of opposition to the government's proposals which transcended party lines and the opposite sides of industry. Four former Secretaries of State for Transport, John Peyton, Richard Marsh, Nicholas Ridley and Barbara Castle; and three former Chairmen of British Rail, Richard Marsh, Peter Parker and Bob Reid, were all on record in opposition to the proposals. Nicholas Ridley, who was Margaret Thatcher's Secretary of State for Transport from 16 October 1983 to 21 May 1986, wrote an article in The Times in December 1992 headed 'Simply no way to run a railway', arguing that the separation of Railtrack from the franchise operators was a recipe for confusion. The Lords Peyton and Marsh, before ennoblement Secretaries of State for Transport from 15 October 1970 to 8 March 1976 and 6 April 1968 to 15 October 1970 respectively, led the opposition to the Bill when it came to the Lords. They were ably backed by Barbara Castle who held similar office under Harold Wilson from 23 December 1965 to 6 April 1968.

The House of Commons all Party Transport Committee heard various key persons' views on the subject of railway privatisation after the appearance of the White Paper, but before the Bill was published and the Second Reading debated. Major General Lennox Napier, the Chairman of the Central Transport Consultative Committee (after privatisation renamed the Central Rail Users Consultative Committee) was heard on 11 November 1992. He said:

> We are thoroughly clear that we would wish to keep the track and infrastructure in public ownership ... if anybody disintegrates the network advantages, the network effect, privatisation will not work, nor will it work unless there is a high level of sustained investment.

He went on to 'vigorously suggest' that BR should be required to bid for all franchises so that there is some opposition or competition, and they should not only bid for them but they should remain as a primary, not just a residual operator, but as a strong competitive provider of train services.[5] Lennox Napier's Committee also submitted a detailed memorandum on numerous issues of railway policy. This included the recommendation that it should be the government's

> responsibility to ensure that there is a continuity in the replacement and upgrading of rolling stock across the entire network.

The White Paper had suggested that one justifiable economy that might be adopted by the Railway Operating Companies would be to make use of 'a healthy second hand market'. The Consultative Committee scorned this proposal:

> This downgrading of equipment is precisely what has happened since bus deregulation; fleet ages have increased enormously, because there is no central body which can order vehicles in sufficient quantity to enable economies of scale to reduce unit prices.[6]

The proposal to allow operating companies 'open access' to all lines was dismissed equally derisively:

> Open access will increase the commercial risks of train operations perceived by private sector franchisees because it will make assessment of market share and operating revenues more uncertain.[7]

It is significant that as a result of this warning and of the hesitations of potential franchisees of operating companies less than a month later John MacGregor announced the abandonment of the plan for open access.[8]

The Local Authority Association, representing County, District and Metropolitan organisations, the Shire Public Transport Consortium and the Convention of Scottish Local Authorities, presented an agreed Memorandum to the Commons Transport Committee, expressing concern that 'unless the government gave more priority to the level of investment and the role of rail in broader land use and environmental strategies it would miss new opportunities rather than create them'.[9]

The Institution of Civil Engineers in its Memorandum to the Transport Committee was similarly concerned whether adequate infrastructure investment would result from the arrangement proposed under the White Paper. It pointed out that British Rail had 'suffered from consistent underinvestment in comparison with the railways of other European countries' and that

> coordination and direction of infrastructure investment, by a body with explicit responsibility for doing so, is an essential function which must be considered more carefully.[10]

The Institution also wanted to see a 'level playing field' between road and rail:

> Cost-benefit appraisal should be applied to all new rail infrastructure investment as it is to all new road schemes, with full recognition given to the environmental benefits of transferring passengers and freight from road to rail and of reducing road congestion. This would help to eliminate distortions in the transport market and establish fair competition between the two modes.[11]

These were authoritative bodies whose disinterested warnings should have been heeded.

The proposals for railway privatisation were also unpopular. A Gallup survey conducted on behalf of the Daily Telegraph – a paper which generally supported Conservative governments – found that 71 per cent of rail users were against the government's plans. Only 18 per cent of those questioned were in favour of privatisation. When passengers were asked for their preference between privatisation and more investment by British Rail, 84 per cent opted for the greater volume of investment and only 9 per cent favoured privatisation.[12]

Meanwhile in a written parliamentary reply John MacGregor announced a reduction of one quarter in BR's grant. The level of investment allowed was to be the lowest since the railways were nationalised in 1948.[13] In consequence the CTCC received a record number of rail-users' complaints in the weeks up to mid-August 1993.[14]

The long drawn out parliamentary process began with the Second Reading debate on the Railways Bill in the House of Commons on 2 February 1993. The proposed measure largely followed the outline given in the White Paper of the previous July.

In moving the Second Reading of the Bill John MacGregor began by attacking the character and performance of BR. He claimed that

it combined the classic shortcomings of the traditional nationalised industry. It is an entrenched monopoly. That means too little responsiveness to customer needs ... Inevitably also it has the culture of a nationalised industry; a heavily bureaucratised structure ... an instinctive tendency to ask for more taxpayers' subsidy.[15]

He claimed that in order to get more freight back on to the rails breaking BR's monopoly was 'crucial'. After explaining the plan to separate the ownership of the track, signalling and stations from the franchisees' job of providing the train services, he said:

'We have now decided that BR ownership of Railtrack' (NB as proposed under the White Paper, P.S.B.) is now no longer necessary or desirable ... Railtrack will be a truly independent, commercially driven body, a government owned body separated from BR in April 1994.'[16]

Separate privately owned companies would run the freight services. He rejected vertical integration, i.e. the franchisees of rail services having ownership of the track and signals. It was neither practical nor desirable because it was inconsistent with the principles of free competition and free access to the tracks. BR would be denied the right to bid for franchises.[17]

In the debate which followed MacGregor's speech there was opposition to the proposed Bill from members of all three of the main political parties. There were contributions from well informed Labour MPs such as John Prescott, who led his party's front bench transport team, and Keith Hill, MP for Streatham and prominent member of the Commons Transport Committee; Nick Harvey, the Liberal Democrat MP for North Devon; Robert Adley, Conservative MP for Christchurch and railway enthusiast; and his colleague from the government benches, David Howell MP for Guildford, who spoke for the stockbroker belt commuters. The concerns they expressed were the danger of increased bureaucracy, the absence of any strategy for investment and future planning of transport; the possible threats to the safety of railway operation and the uncertainty about the frequency of services and the concessions made to elderly and young persons' travel.

The most brazen claim made by MacGregor was that the government's proposals would lead to a decrease in bureaucracy. He made this claim not only in his opening remarks but later on as well when he asserted

When the new system is up and running it will be more streamlined and less bureaucratic than the previous system.[18]

In challenging this claim John Prescott cited Harold Davies, the Director General of the CBI, who believed that

there is a real danger that privatisation will be a blueprint for bureaucracy.[19]

Keith Hill pointed out that the government was creating 'a quagmire of quangoes which would form a veritable minefield of day to day conflict'.[20] Nick Harvey drew parallels from the experience of bus deregulation and the confusion and loss of services it created.[21]

The critics were agreed that vastly increased investment in the railway system was necessary. David Howell, whose constituents lived in the Network SouthEast area, were looking for

a wholly new enhanced and dedicated transport service for the area. This will require vast investment funds.[22]

Robert Adley questioned:

From where is the investment to come for Railtrack? Who is to finance the new railway? There is no mention of any investment regime in the Bill. Investment is fundamental ... [23] There has been a total lack of any coherent transport policy during the past 14 years which has caused the problem. The hostility of the government under Lady Thatcher to anything in the public sector forms the background to today's Bill.[24]

John MacGregor in reply claimed that investment levels were 'the highest since thirty years ago' and that there was a prospect of 'investment through revenue' and more private capital to come in.[25] John Prescott pointed out that MacGregor's figure as 'the highest since thirty years ago' was inflated through private investment in the Channel Tunnel and Keith Hill reminded the House that in 1994 investment in the existing railway would fall to half the 1993 level.

On the matter of the safety of railway operation John Prescott cited the Health and Safety Executive's warning that

> Companies with little or no previous experience of operating on the railway and managers with little experience of railway safety issues, will enter the railway industry as the BR monopoly is broken. Unless considerable care is taken to set up systems to ensure that new operators are properly equipped and organised, there can be no confidence that risk will be effectively controlled right from the start, and that important matters do not fall between the safety arrangements of various parties.[26]

Robert Adley made the common sense comment that

> The more people who are involved in safety the more safety is jeopardised.[27]

Despite these expressions of concern party loyalty prevailed. The Second Reading of the Bill was carried by 303 votes to 269. Only one other Conservative sat with Robert Adley in abstaining from voting.

Those MPs who still had their doubts about the Bill hoped to amend it in the Committee stage which followed the Second Reading. It took no less than 35 sessions to consider the 250 amendments tabled by both government and opposition. The Bill as amended was debated on the night of 25 May and was carried by 307 votes to 292. The government won because it made some concessions to the backbench rebels led by Sir Keith Speed. MacGregor promised that concessionary railcards for the young, elderly and disabled would be granted by amendments in the Lords. He conceded that the franchising director should be given powers to control fares to ensure that any rises were reasonable. Those who were worried about the inadequate level of investment were mollified by a new requirement, that the Department of Transport should publish an investment plan in its annual report.[28]

On one important issue, however, MacGregor refused to give way to the opposition and his own backbench rebels. Under

Clause 22 neither BR nor any of its subsidiary organisations was to be allowed to bid for any of the franchises.

It was on this question that the Lords crossed swords with the government when the Bill came before the Upper House on 5 July 1993. All of the former Secretaries of State for Transport were decisive in their opposition to the plan to exclude BR from any part in running the new railway. Lord Peyton moved an amendment to Clause 22

> Nothing in subsection (1) above shall prevent (a) the British Railways Board ... or (b) a wholly owned subsidiary of the Board, from being a franchisee.

He said

> The amendment would let British Rail in. In effect it would be a step back from the clear intention of the Bill to kill off BR and bury the corpse at an early date.

He criticised the government's proposals more generally:

> The organisation and its components will produce an immense complexity of relationships, a cobweb of regulations, rules, licences, agreements and memoranda which are bound to come into existence. Inevitably there will be conflicts, disputes and misunderstandings.[29]

Lord Marsh found the problem with the Bill was that it was 'motivated overwhelmingly by pure, blind, unthinking dogma'.[30] Baroness Castle noted that until then

> nobody [had] suggested that the public sector should be excluded from showing whether it could compete on merit. It was a total tyranny to brand BR a failure as the noble Lord (the Earl of Caithness) had done. He does not wish it to be allowed to prove whether it can compete. That is a level playing field for you in true Tory terms.[31]

Lord Clinton Davis cited other government bodies, such as the NHS and London Underground, which were allowed to bid under the competitive tendering system and in 75 per cent of the cases 'in house' bidding had been successful.

> 'In this Bill', he said, 'the government want to have private investment regardless of whether it will

improve the railway system and benefit consumers. It is an absurd situation'.[32]

The Earl of Caithness put the government's case for the Bill and against Lord Peyton's amendment. He repeated the general case for privatisation made in the Lower House.

We believe that the best way to produce profound and lasting improvements in the railways is to end BR's state monopoly. ... Experience shows that the private sector is generally more responsive, more flexible, more innovative and more efficient.

The government favoured management pay-outs and said that it would reimburse costs on the scale of 85 per cent of the first £10,00 and 75 per cent up to an overall maximum of £100,000. He was firmly against BR being allowed to bid for franchises.

Allowing BR to bid would undermine private sector interest because BR would be bidding on the basis of access to capital at preferential rates, due to the implicit government guarantee that it would have ... Many in the private sector would probably think they were wasting their money in even preparing a bid against BR.[33]

He did not mention that SJ, the Swedish state owned railway, had been allowed to bid against private companies for operating rail services and had won over 95 per cent of the contracts, a fact which had been pointed out to both John Prescott and Robert Adley in the Commons' debate.

Lord Peyton was successful in carrying this most important of the hundreds of amendments to the Railways Bill proposed in the Upper House. Enough Tory, Liberal and cross bench peers supported the Labour group in favour of the amendment for Lord Peyton to carry the day by 150 votes to 112.

During the summer recess there was widespread talk in the Commons and among journalists that John Major was on the point of abandoning the Bill. The Independent on Sunday carried a front page banner headline Major ready for rail retreat[34] while the Financial Times headline read: Defeat in Lords threatens sell-off BR.[35] They both reckoned without Patrick Brown, Permanent Secretary of the Department of Transport, who was described as being of the 'find a solution and make it work' school. He had steered through the privatisations of buses, ports and water and urged Major who had visited prominent Conservative Lords and thought about a face saving formula to stand firm against the anti-privateers.[36] MacGregor therefore stood his ground and marked time.

It was not until 1 November that the Commons considered the Lords' amendments. In the last fortnight of October a number of Conservative MPs had been urging MacGregor either to accept the Lords' amendment giving BR the right to bid for franchises or to accept a compromise.[37] These rebels were without the leadership of Robert Adley who had died of a heart attack at the early age of 58 on 13 April. As the obituary in the Financial Times observed, his death left the unease among Tory backbenchers 'without a clear focus or spokesman'.[38]

With severely limited time in which to consider the Lords' amendments because of the government's passing of a guillotine motion, the Commons debated what had become known as the 'Peyton amendment' early in the evening of 2 November. MacGregor had earlier promised the Lords that he would need to amend the Peyton amendment to improve its wording. It transpired that he changed it so as to deny the right of BR to bid for franchises except in cases were there was no other bidder. Keith Hill and other speakers stressed that the government were fearful that if BR were allowed to bid it would win most of the franchises. Nevertheless the government won the day and the Bill was returned to the Lords.[39]

The Upper House considered the Commons' treatment of Lord Peyton's other amendments on the following evening, 3 November, in the knowledge that every word of the 243 page Bill had to be agreed by both houses by the following morning, 4 November, the end of the session, if it was to survive. Failing agreement, it would disappear and a new Bill would have to be presented in the following session.

Lord Marsh moved an amendment to the Commons' amendment which would have restored the right of BR to bid for franchises. Lord Harmer Nicholls expressed the view that

>having sent this matter once to another place, they
>should give the government the benefit of the doubt and
>accept their advice,[40]

but Lord Tordoff said that they <u>did</u> have the right 'to ask the
other place to consider the matter again and again'. They had
that right under the Parliament Act and Lord Clinton Davis
angrily asserted that

>what the government have done – is to produce an
>~~amendment which is a blatant attempt to subvert the~~
>amendment of the noble Lord, Lord Peyton. ... The
>truth is that BR has been put in a position that it can
>bid only when no one else wants to do so. Nothing has
>changed.[41]

At this stage the anti-government Lords carried the day. Lord
Marsh's amendment was approved by 170 to 160 votes. After
dealing with other amendments the sitting was suspended to give
time for the Commons to react to the above-mentioned resolution.
In the light of the fact that the Commons was the democratically
elected assembly, the House of Lords surrendered to the Commons'
decisions at 11.30pm on Wednesday 3 November and the Bill
received the Queen's signature on 5 November 1993.[42] The Act
came into force on 1 April 1994.

The Railways Act, 1993, confirmed the division between the
organisation Railtrack which owned the track, stations and signals,
and the 25 operating companies. Railtrack's status was finally
determined by a ministerial statement at a later date. The
Franchising Director Opraf is responsible for advising the
Secretary of State on the granting of franchises to train
operators and for allocating the government's PSO grant. The
Rail Regulator is charged with ensuring that the interests of all
associated with the railway, both customers and operators, are
given the best possible service. Many details of the working of
the Act were settled by the Secretary of State for Transport after
1 April 1994.

Nevertheless a great many questions were left unanswered.
Peter Snape, MP asked some very pertinent questions of the
Secretary of State on 25 February 1992. He questioned how
many civil servants would be employed enforcing the hundreds

of new regulations which would arise, especially the regulations regarding safety, and whether the cost of their employment would be met by the Exchequer or railway customers. He wanted to know which authority would have responsibility for the safety training of staff and testing their professional competence. How did he intend to be responsible for the introduction of automatic train control over the system and how would essential safety expenditure be financed; who would be responsible for research and development, and who would represent British railways on the International Union of Railways; what contribution would be made to the Railway Heritage Trust, and who would represent British railways in matters relating to the Channel Tunnel. Roger Freeman, the Minister for Public Transport, answered vaguely 'We shall make known our proposals in due course',[43] but on 1 April 1994 when the Railways Bill came into operation a lot of these questions were still not adequately answered.

Chapter Thirteen: **Notes**

1. Commons, Hansard, 6th ser. vol.187, 13 March 1991, col.1072.
2. Ibid., col.1075.
3. The Times Guide to the House of Commons, April 1992, (1992), p.318.
4. Ibid., p.329.
5. House of Commons Transport Committee, 11 November 1992, para.420.
6. Central Transport Consultative Committee, Memorandum to the House of Commons Transport Committee, 11 November 1992, Section 8, Rolling Stock.
7. Ibid., Section A2.2.
8. Financial Times, 8 December 1992.
9. Submission of Local Authority Associations to the Commons Transport Committee, The Future Prospects for the Railway System in the light of the Government's proposals for Privatisation, (16 December 1992).
10. Memorandum submitted by the Institution of Civil Engineers to the Commons Transport Committee, 11 November 1992, para. 4.

11. Ibid., para. 4.4
12. Daily Telegraph, 22 May 1993.
13. Commons, Hansard, 6th ser. vol.222, 30 March 1993, cols.163-5.
14. Sunday Times, 22 August 1993.
15. Commons, Hansard, 6th ser. vol.218, 27 February 1993, col.156.
16. Ibid., col.161
17. Ibid., col.165
18. Ibid., col.173
19. Ibid., col.180
20. Ibid., col.205
21. Ibid., col.191
22. Ibid., col.160
23. Ibid., col.204
24. Ibid., col.218
25. Ibid., col.161
26. Ibid., col.184
27. Idem.
28. Railnews, June 1993, p.8.
29. Lords, Hansard, vol.547 no.164, 5 July 1993, cols.1069-70.
30. Ibid., col.1076
31. Ibid., cols.1081-2
32. Ibid., col.1072
33. Ibid., col.1095, Commons, Hansard, 6th ser. vol.218, 2 February 1993, cols. 180 and 205.
34. The Independent on Sunday, 29 August 1993.
35. Financial Times, 6 July 1993.
36. Jeremy Warner, 'Rail sell-off could still be on track', Independent on Sunday, 29 August 1993.
37. Financial Times, 19 October 1993.
38. Financial Times, 14 April 1993.
39. Commons, Hansard, 6th ser. vol.231, col.288.
40. Lords, Hansard, vol.549, 3 November 1993, col.1098.
41. Ibid., col.1100
42. Ibid., 5 November 1993, col.1183.
43. Commons, Hansard, 6th ser. vol.204, col.480.

Chapter Fourteen
The Costs of
Rail Privatisation

There were short term and longer term costs of railway privatisation. At the time of the Railways Bill enactment on 1 April 1994 the most authoritative estimate of the costs of privatisation thus far was £649 million made by the all-party Public Accounts Committee.[1] The Department of Transport supplied to Brian Wilson MP, a Labour frontbench spokesman, the breakdown of this huge figure: £303 million was spent on 13,114 staff redundancies and early retirements; £146 million for restructuring in 1992-3; £100 million for integrating new systems; £48 million in fees to legal, financial, public relations and other advisers; £32 million to create the railway franchise organisation Opraf, and £20 million to establish the rail regulation system Ofrail. After the disclosure of these figures Brian Wilson declared that the £649 million total was practically the same as the £650 million capital investment needed for the long-overdue modernisation of the west coast main line from London to Glasgow (a route, incidentally, which is only eight miles longer than that from London to Edinburgh, but a journey which takes an hour longer to complete). Three Labour MPs, Michael Meacher, Henry Mcleish and Glenda Jackson, in their pamphlet Runaway Train (1995) by including other costs, such as pension payments due, put the estimate of the cost of the transition to private ownership as high as £1,250 million.

The British taxpayer was saddled with additional expense through the fact that, accompanying privatisation, the Public Service Obligation grant from the Treasury to the railways was nearly doubled, from £930 million in 1993-4 to £1.74 million in 1994-5.[2] There was widespread concern both in the Commons and in the country at large that privatisation would lead to the operating companies raising fares – so that they could meet Railtrack's charges for the use of the track – at the same time as paying an acceptable return to their shareholders. In May 1995 Mr Roger Salmon, the franchising director, reassured critics that service levels and fares would be maintained. To mollify the operating companies Mr Brian Mawhinney, the Secretary of State for Transport, stated during a BBC <u>On the Record</u> programme, that he would provide 'necessary and appropriate' levels of subsidy to enable them to meet service requirements demanded by Roger Salmon.[3] Potential investors and serving managers of operating companies had been encouraged by the earlier relaxation by the Treasury of the rules for Railtrack charges. Initially that organisation was urged to generate enough revenue to earn an 8 per cent return on capital. However, would-be investors in the operating companies were reluctant to come forward if they had to meet such high access charges. Therefore, in January 1994 Mawhinney declared that Railtrack would need to gain only 5 per cent in the initial years after privatisation, though thereafter its target would rise in stages to 8 per cent.[4] Mr Swift, the Rail Regulator, claimed that the cut in rail access charges 'would achieve a better balance of advantage between all the parties operating in the new railway market'.[5]

But the easing of financial requirements of the operating companies meant, to that extent, less revenue for Railtrack, prompting Robert Horton, the company's chairman, to go cap in hand to the Treasury pleading for the reduction of his concern's inherited debt by £1.6 billion. Horton had a bargaining lever over the government. He knew that John Major's cabinet was keen to collect the revenue from the sale of Railtrack during the lifetime of parliament and that an attractive price would have to be offered to investors for the sale to be successful. In the negotiations the government at first threatened to abandon Railtrack's privatisation if the debt reduction was more than £600 million. However, in the end, a debt reduction of £1 billion was agreed, and this, in the words of the <u>Financial Times</u> headline, 'cleared the way for the sale of Railtrack'.[6] Thus a billion pounds of public (Treasury) money was handed over to a private company, in contrast to the earlier starving of the publicly owned BR of much needed money for investment in infrastructure and rolling stock.

It is not surprising that the sale of Railtrack shares on 20 May 1996 was oversubscribed. In the first case the prospectus, issued a few days before the sale, was too one-sided.

John Welsby, Chairman of the British Railways Board, in a
letter to Sir Patrick Brown, permanent secretary at the
Department of Transport, sent on 2 April 1996, wrote[7] that the
prospectus did not give a 'fair view of the vulnerabilities' of the
business. Regarding Railtrack's performance, he warned that he
had 'serious concerns about the service offered on the line in and
out of Euston'. He criticised the prospectus for failing to
mention 'a significant downturn in performance' of a number of
operating companies in the early months of 1996 and claimed
that this was 'surely material information for investors'.

The government was so desperate to ensure the financial
success of the sale of Railtrack that it allowed a £69 million
'sweetener' to investors on its flotation. The prospectus stated
that investors could not only expect a good dividend for the
financial year 1996-7 but also an unprecedented extra one – the
£69 million – for the previous financial year 1995-6 when
Railtrack was still publicly owned. In other words, the
£69 million, which should have gone to the Exchequer, would go
to the new private shareholders. This sum should therefore be
added to the earlier estimates of the costs of privatisation.

In the British Railways Board Annual Report and Accounts
for 1994/5 the Board's auditors stated that the gross value of
'buildings and infrastructure' (i.e. stations, signal boxes, offices
and the track) was £6,464 million as at 1 April 1994.[8] But at
the sale on 20 May 1996 Railtrack's assets were given as
£1.9 billion, an outrageously low figure, fixed to ensure that
purchasers of shares would be offered an exceptionally good
bargain which would guarantee a return of anything from 13 to
20 per cent in the first financial year. The enormity of this
downgrading of an essential public asset can be seen when it is
realised that the Major government sold off the entire rail
network of 23,494 miles of track, 2,615 stations, and signalling,
for less than the £2.1 billion needed for the projected Cross Rail
link from Paddington to Liverpool Street in London.[9] It is no
wonder that the privatised Railtrack saw its shares soar from
their offer price to the small investor of 190p to 229p within
hours of the launch. This represented a profit of £78 for an
investor with the minimum holding of £300.[10]

A little-noticed part of the Railtrack prospectus offered directors and senior executives cash bonuses, part of which could be converted into shares, which in turn could qualify them for additional free shares. By this means, in the most favourable circumstances, they could get an additional 20 per cent of their salaries, plus shares worth five times their salaries (which range from £98,470 to £154,500 per annum). This roundabout method of rewarding top executives, in contrast to the policy of awarding lump sum bonuses, would reduce the likelihood of 'fat cats' allegations such as were made against British Gas.[11]

Although the unscrupulous waste of public assets was manifest in the case of the sale of Railtrack, an even bigger scandal occurred in the government's record over the construction of the rail link to the Channel Tunnel. On 12 February 1986 Margaret Thatcher and President Mitterrand of France signed in Canterbury, Kent, a treaty for the construction of the Channel Tunnel.[12] This had followed a joint ceremony held at Lille, northern France, on 20 January that year. Though both the heads of state were agreed on the advantages of a rail rather than a road link, for technical and organisational reasons, they had different approaches to the problem of financing this gigantic enterprise. From the start Margaret Thatcher made it abundantly clear that both the construction of the tunnel and of the rail approaches to it on the British side would have to be entirely privately financed. The tradition in France was of the value of support for infrastructure works being financed in greater part from public funds. Margaret Thatcher's last Secretary of State for Transport, Cecil Parkinson, declared unequivocally in 1990 that, under the Channel Tunnel Act of 1987, 'it would be illegal for the government to provide money for the rail link'. However, the Thatcher and Major governments' stubborn adherence to the belief, that all great works of public utility had to be privately financed, produced long delays until a final crisis was reached in the first two months of 1996. No bank, group of banks, or consortium of entrepreneurs could be found to construct the 68 mile rail link to the capital without very substantial 'sweeteners' from the government. Eventually the Major government had to give in. In January and February 1996 it became clear that a consortium, the London and Continental, had agreed with Sir George Young, the Secretary of State for Transport, acting on behalf of the government, to a contract for building the rail link. Under this contract the Tory government, which, together with its predecessor for more than a decade had refused to commit any public funds to such an enterprise, undertook to provide a subsidy of £1.4 billion towards the estimated £3 billion construction costs of the Channel Tunnel Rail Link (CTRL) between Folkestone and St. Pancras. The consortium, whose main participants were Virgin, National Express and S.B.C. Warburg, were to receive, in addition, public assets worth a total estimated at £5.7 billion, of which the principal elements were the Waterloo International station (£500 m); 120 acres of prime central London land (£3 billion); St. Pancras Chambers, a 250-bed hotel (£70 m); Eurostar trains and other rolling stock (£65 m) and the residue comprising St. Pancras Station, 635 separate properties and 120 acres in East London.[13] One transport analyst described the whole package as 'the mother of all sweeteners'. It was the greatest exposure of the falsity of the claim that the Private Finance Initiative was the more efficient and economical way of funding great public utility enterprises than that of funding through government loans.

Labour's frontbench spokesperson on transport, Clare Short, dubbed the deal with London and Continental as the 'great asset give away' and declared that 'British Rail could have built the line seven years ago for less than £1.9 billion of public money'.[14] Under the contract, the consortium undertook to complete the rail link by the year 2002, a decade later than the rail link on the French side of the Channel Tunnel had been completed. In mid May 1996 the French President, M. Chirac, paid an official visit to London, coming from Paris by Eurostar. It would be interesting to know his thoughts on the Private Finance Initiative after travelling to the French entrance to the tunnel at 186 miles an hour and proceeding from Folkestone through Kent on a more bumpy ride at a third of that speed!

To sum up the financial costs of rail privatisation we have the following items:

TABLE 5 Financial Costs of Rail Privatisation

	£ m.
Costs associated with the launching of the Railways Act	650
Increase in P.S.O. grant needed	818
Debt reduction for Railtrack	1,000
'Sweeteners' to Railtrack shareholders	69
Undervaluation of Railtrack's assets (a conservative estimate)	3,000
London and Continental for tunnel rail link	5,700
TOTAL £ billion	11,437

And, it must be remembered, it was John MacGregor who had accused British Rail of 'an instinctive tendency to ask for more taxpayer's subsidy'![15]

In the summer of 1991 Bob Reid, the British Railways Board Chairman, set out in the publication Future Rail 'a Ten Year Programme of investment in assets and people' with a price tag of upwards £1 billion a year.[16] Had the £11 billion which the Major government squandered in the privatisation programme been made available to BR, the railway system could have been in tip top condition by the start of the new millennium.

In April 1994 when Railtrack took over the track, signalling and stations from BR, it announced 'that it planned to make substantial cuts in the maintenance and repair bills.[17] This enabled it to declare pre-tax profits of over £180 million in September 1995.[18] The Commons all Party Transport Committee was suspicious. In its report of 5 July 1995 it commended the Railway Regulator and Railtrack for agreeing that the rail infrastructure needed to spend about £510 million a year to catch up with serious arrears in track renewal and modernisation of signalling. However, from the Railway Industries Association it received evidence that 'orders from Railtrack for signalling and track components had fallen steeply since Railtrack was formed', and that 'purchases of rails, rail fastenings and switches had declined in the previous two years to well below the average of European railways'. In its Summary of Conclusions and Recommendations it lambasted Railtrack for its 'failure to publish the Ten Year Strategy which it promised to parliament during the passage of the 1993 Railways Act'. It also found 'a cause for concern' the size of 'the gap between the perceptions of Railtrack and the Railway Industries Association's members as to the volume of signalling work actually taking place'.[19]

It is understandable in the light of Railtrack Chairman's statement that he planned to make 'substantial cuts in maintenance and repair bills' that there was a growing concern about the safety of railway operation. The Commons Transport Committee reported that it had been informed by the Institute of Railway Signal Engineers that

the age and safety of electrical signalling introduced in the 1950s and 1960s was causing concern. Lack of finance would appear to have delayed both renewal and improvement to these safety systems and the current indications are that this situation will worsen.

The same committee noted that 'during the first eighteen months of rail privatisation track replacement had fallen to an average of 1.1 per cent per annum, which would mean that rails had reached a predictable life of over 90 years'. It conceded that 'even British Steel admit that is not possible'.[20]

Robert Horton's statement that he had scope to make substantial cuts was highly questionable. As Owen Simon wrote in the Financial Times:

BR operates one of the leanest railways in Europe and scope for internal efficiency savings is small.[21]

In consequence railway staff were being pressurised to take risks. In September 1995 Jack Rose, Safety Assistant Manager at Railtrack, declared that safety provision was in such a bad state that 'lives could be at risk', while Vernon Hince, Assistant General Secretary of the Rail, Maritime and Transport Workers Union (RMT), wrote:

There have been a number of instances when safety representatives, who have challenged working arrangements, have been threatened with disciplinary action and dismissal.[22]

Critics of railway privatisation have repeatedly warned that the splitting of BR into more than 80 private companies and the conflict they are bound to experience between the need to economise to make funds available for the payment of dividends to their shareholders and the demands for safe methods of operation will lead to the greater risk of accidents. Karen Harrison, a delegate from ASLEF at the Annual Women's Conference of the TUC on 14 March 1996 warned:

> Railtrack has no incentive to keep the tracks in good condition – it will be like a slum landlord taking the money but failing to maintain and improve the facilities.[23]

On 7 March 1996 the Railway Inspectorate, part of the Health and Safety Executive, published a critical report of Railtrack's procedures following a four-month HSE investigation. On one occasion a driver reported that he had been unable to see a trackside signal. Maintenance staff subsequently discovered that the signal had been removed and not replaced by another contractor. The HSE Report concluded:

> We did find weaknesses in the way that Railtrack seeks to maintain health and safety. Shortcomings in formal management systems do not necessarily lead directly to accidents, but they can eat away at safety margins and they can lead to an increase in the risk of harm.[24]

In the months since Railtrack took over responsibility for track signalling and stations from BR there have been serious accidents such as those at Cowden in Kent in October 1994 when there were five fatalities, on the line from Barking to Gospel Oak, London, on 18 February 1985 when 31 persons were injured and when one person was killed, and many more narrowly escaped serious injury or death in a collision between a tanker train and a Royal Mail express near Stafford on 8 March 1996. However the trend in the number of fatalities was downwards compared with previous years.[25] What was alarming was the rise in the number of 'near misses' which rarely received public notice. The Commons Transport Committee declared that Railtrack was too secretive about these incidents and on 13 March 1996 Railtrack responded by promising to provide

156

more information.[26] However, alarm was expressed when on June 4 following, the government issued a 'gagging order' for three months until August 1 on public bodies, forbidding them from making statements which could adversely affect the price of shares of Railtrack so soon after its flotation on 20 May. Critics claimed that vital information was being withheld from BR, the HSE, the Railway Regulator and the Franchising Director, because the government wished to hide the facts about deficiencies in safety measures.[27]

If doubts were expressed about the adequacy of Railtrack's maintenance performance, there could be no doubt about the decline in investment in the railways in the approach to and the aftermath of the passing of the Railways Act in 1993.

Figure 11 shows that railway investment fell from £1,059 million in 1991-2, through £1,004 in 1992-3, and £663 million in 1993-4 to £490 million in 1994-5. In the Commons Michael Meacher MP described this as 'a staggering cut of 54 per cent in three years'.[28]

FIG.11 UK Public Investment in railways 1991-1995

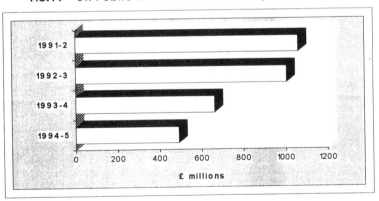

Source: Commons Hansard, 6th ser. vol.260, 17 May 1995, col.342 and vol.261, 6 June 1995, cols.49-50. Written answers to questions by Michael Meacher, MP.

None of Mr MacGregor's claims was more ridiculous than that the privatised railway he was proposing would release the UK from the 'heavily bureaucratised structure' of BR.[29] In fact BR's organisation was simplicity itself compared with the confused jungle of organisations set up under the Railways Act. Under the new regime every station with more than one railway company user – and by 1995 there were an estimated 94 company organisations involved – needed a 42 page lease and a 196 page station access document. Every user requires a collateral contract of 26 pages and a 31 page station access agreement. Since there are 2615 stations, these changes can be seen as good news for the paper industry, but scarcely a step on the road towards the elimination of bureaucracy. In an interview with Charles Batchelor on the completion of his five years' leadership of the British Railways Board Sir Bob Reed feared that

> a paperwork mountain will become a permanent feature of the railways, distracting managers from running an efficient service.

He did not believe that this mountain would disappear once the privatisation process had been completed. 'The bureaucracy is endemic', he said, 'every question raises five more'.[30]

A casualty of the early stages of rail privatisation was the railway construction industry. The uncertainties about the future structure of the railway industry and the dates for the completion of the various stages of privatisation caused BR, Railtrack and the Train Operating Units (TOUs) to defer investment in rolling stock and track renewals. BR made drastic reductions in its orders for new rolling stock in the financial years 1992-93 and 1993-94 and no calls for tender in 1994-95 until 21 March 1995, when tenders to build about 40 Networkers were invited. However, neither of the two companies tendering submitted a satisfactory bid. The result was that ABB Transportation of York, Britain's biggest train builder, lacking any orders, sacked almost 900 workers in June 1993.[31] Mercifully, BR felt able by February 1995 to afford the 40 Networkers. In a letter to ABB and GEC-Alsthom (another rolling stock manufacturer) BR stated that the order would be placed 'in recognition of the order position of the two rolling stock manufacturers'. This offered some hope to ABB and the 750 men still employed in its York works.[32]

By the time the first six TOC franchises had been sold by Roger Salmon, the Franchising Director, it became clear that the three largest bus companies, Stagecoach, First Bus and National Express, had obtained the lion's share. The situation at the end of April 1996 is summed up as follows:

TABLE 6 The First Six Railway Operating Franchises

Franchise	Winner	Period (years)	New Rolling Stock	Subsidy
South West Trains	Stagecoach	7	No	Yes
Great Western	First Bus/Management	10	Possibly	Yes
East Coast Main Line	Sea Containers	7	No	Yes[1]
Gatwick Express	National Express	15	Yes	No
Network South Central	CGEA (France)	7	No	Yes
Midland Main Line	National Express	10	Yes	Yes[2]

Notes (1) Subsidy reducing to zero. (2) Subsidy becomes payment by MML in 2000.[33]

Both Railtrack and some of the new operating companies showed initiative in stressing the importance of good staff relations with passengers (or, to use the new 'in' word 'customers'). Staff at NorthEast Trains based in York wear blue uniforms with yellow buttons and borders to their coats and yellow bands round their headgear. Facial appearance is considered important. Beards are banned at Manchester but 'neatly trimmed facial hair' is allowed on the Transpennine Express. Merseyrail and Anglia have issued pocket-sized codes telling staff when to smile at passengers and whether to address them as 'mate' or 'pet'. Saying 'I can't help you' is banned. Midland Main Line staff have been advised to introduce 'American style friendliness' into their voices.[34]

Smart appearance of staff and their willingness to answer questions (which, incidentally, the author has in the past found to be the case with BR staff) are no substitute for serving the best interests of the passengers, rather than the interest of the private railway company. The departure indicator at Euston, which belongs to Railtrack, lists two sorts of passenger trains going to Birmingham without indicating that one of them is a stopping, slow, train provided by the TOC North London Railways and the other is an InterCity West Coast Express still run by British Rail, the more frequent and faster service of the two. But, clearly, the interests of the private company were put before those of the passenger.[35] Passengers wanting an accurate timetable for the route they intend to follow will often find it more difficult to obtain the information they require because of the splintering of BR into 25 operating companies. The ROC's pocket timetables will show the trains on their territory, but not the further destinations on to other companies' lines. The timetables for trains heading north out of Newcastle in BR days used to include the service between Newcastle and Berwick, showing both InterCity and Regional Railways trains. Since privatisation, however, Regional Railways North East's timetable shows trains only as far as Chathill, the northern limit of its area, even though all the trains go on to Berwick.[36] Dozens more illustrations could be provided of the obstacles to efficient operation of passenger and freight services arising as a result of the fragmentation of BR.

Under the Passenger's Charter issued by BR in 1989 punctuality targets were set for the arrival of trains, and when services fell short of these by more than a permitted margin passengers could claim financial compensation. The Charter still is recognized but two significant changes have been made. The journey times shown on timetables have been extended to make it easier for operators to reach targets set and it is infinitely harder to obtain satisfactory compensation because it is much easier to 'pass the buck' of responsibility for delay from one company to another or from one (or more) company/companies to Railtrack.

Perhaps the most serious consequence of privatisation is the decline in the number of meaningful jobs. Railway labour is regarded by the new profit-oriented ROCs as a cost. When applying for franchises bidders vie with each other in claiming that they can perform the tasks set them by the franchise director with fewer members of staff than can rival bidders. But railway employment is a service to the travelling public, not a cost of production such as is incurred in manufacturing chairs or videos. Tens of thousands more railway employees are needed to extend the electrified rail network, improve track and signalling safety, and staff the less important stations as well as the mainline termini so ostentatiously displayed to the media.

The number of staff employed in planning, maintaining the infrastructure and running trains in the UK fell from 129,696 in the year ending 31 March 1990 to 94,344 in the year to 31 March 1995, a decrease of 35,352 or nearly 27 per cent over five years.[37] Most of those 35,352 staff could have been usefully employed making the railway service safer, more efficient and welcoming to passengers and the business community.

In view of the predominance of purely commercial consideration under railway privatisation, and the multiplication of the number of separate companies all looking for easy pickings to bolster their financial balances, the railway trade unions needed to be extra vigilant on behalf of their members' pension rights. The RMT urged the introduction of an industrywide pension scheme as the only means of protecting pension rights for all concerned. The White Paper New Opportunities for the Railways, published in July 1992, promised that pensions would not be adversely affected by privatisation. But under the governments' consultation paper it was suggested that pensioners should be offered one of two alternatives. The first was that pensioners and accumulated assets should be transferred to a closed scheme; but this was found unacceptable as future pensions would depend on the success of fund investments. The second option was that appropriate assets should be transferred to the government which would guarantee index-linking, but there would be no prospect of additional improvements. The amounts which would be transferred to the Treasury would be up to £4.25 billion pounds and it was feared that there would be a temptation for funds to be 'raided' for other purposes.

At the time when the government was afraid of the defeat of the Railways Bill in early November 1993 the Minister for Transport agreed a Memorandum of Understanding with the chairman of the Trustees of the Pension Fund. It required continued and intense lobbying in both the Commons and the Lords to ensure the indefeasible right to the Joint Industry Scheme membership when members were transferred from one company within the industry to another. It was a notable, prolonged action by the unions which protected members' rights to the pensions towards which they had contributed.[38]

Chapter Fourteen: Notes

1. Observer, Business supplement, 1 May 1994. The Guardian, 2 May 1994.
2. British Railways Board, Annual Report and Accounts 1994-5, p.54.
3. Financial Times, 15 May 1995.
4. Financial Times, 1 January 1994. Railnews, No.384, February 1995.
5. The Guardian, 18 January 1995.
6. Financial Times, 28 February 1996.
7. Financial Times, 3 April 1996.
8. British Railways Board, Annual Report and Accounts 1994-5, p.59. On 1 January 1994 the Financial Times estimated Railtrack's replacement cost as £7 billion.
9. The Guardian, 16 April 1996. BR, Rail facts and figures 1992, p.10.
10. Paul Corry, in Morning Star, 20 June 1996.
11. Financial Times, 16 April 1996.
12. The Times, 13 February 1986.
13. The Observer, Business, 7 January 1996; Sunday Times, 14 January, 1996; The Guardian, 1 and 4 March 1996.
14. The Guardian, 1 March 1996.
15. Commons, Hansard 6th ser. vol.218, 2 February 1993, col.156.
16. British Railways Board, Future Rail, 1991. Annual Report and Accounts 1992-3, Chairman's Statement, p.6.
17. Financial Times, 27 April 1995.
18. Sunday Times, Business supplement, 3 September 1995.
19. House of Commons Transport Committee, Fourth Report Railway Finances, 5 July 1995, §§ 162-64, p.8.
20. Ibid., conclusions 'o' and 'p', p.liv.
21. Financial Times, 18 March 1994.
22. RMT News, October 1995, p.7.

23. Morning Star, 15 March 1996.
24. Health and Safety Executive, Maintaining a Safe Railway System, (1996).
25. British Railways Board, Annual Report and Accounts 1994-5, p.10.
26. Financial Times, 14 March 1996.
27. The Guardian, 5 June 1996.
28. Commons, Hansard, 6th ser. vol.260, 17 May 1995, col.342.
29. Ibid., vol.218, 2 February 1993, col.156.
30. Financial Times, 31 March 1995.
31. Independent, 8 June 1993.
32. Financial Times, 5 February 1995.
33. Charles Batchelor, 'Railway sell-off picks up speed', Financial Times, 23 April 1996.
34. The Sunday Times, 28 May 1995.
35. Christian Wolmar, The Great British Railway Disaster, (1996) p.50.
36. Ibid., p.56. This book, published by Independent on Sunday, is invaluable for its revelation of the anomalies and the obstacles to passenger and freight services arising from the fragmentation of BR.
37. British Railways Board, Annual Report and Accounts 1994-5.
38. RMT General Secretary's Report, 1993, pp.23-4, and 1994, pp.27-8. Also information kindly supplied by N. Coles.

Chapter Fifteen
Future Policy
(a) Railways

The chapters in Part Two of this book examined the attempts in parliament to tackle the transport problem by legislating for one mode largely in isolation from the others. In 1955 John Boyd-Carpenter, the Minister of Transport and Civil Aviation, backed the British Transport Commission's Modernisation Plan in the belief that, if steam power was replaced by diesel or electric traction, train services would be faster and more reliable, enabling them to challenge more effectively the growing predominance of motorised transport. It was a misconception. Instead, the railways went into an <u>operational</u> and not merely a <u>financial</u> deficit. The MacMillan cabinet believed that the BTC was top heavy in structure, so opted for administrative changes. In 1962 the Commission was abolished and different organisations for rail, road transport and inland waterways were created. The belief that by cutting off the unprofitable feeder and secondary lines from the railway network it would bring the residue back into profit, as tried out under the Beeching Plan of 1963, was shown to be fallacious. Under the Transport Act of 1968 it was hoped that by singling out the socially necessary, but financially unprofitable, lines and supporting them by government grant, the main 8,000 mile network would become profitable, and that through the creation of the National Freight Corporation the railways would secure a larger proportion of the long distance carriage of goods and raw materials. For a few years after 1968 the financial position of BR improved, but the seemingly inexorable decline in its share of the traffic continued.

From 1979 under the Thatcher and Major governments the philosophy of the free market, deregulation and freedom from government control has been dominant. The bus industry was freed under the Transport Acts of 1980 and 1985, but their passage resulted in a reduction of public transports' share of total road passenger movement. Finally the Railways Act of 1993 broke up BR's domain through the creation of dozens of railway operating and manufacturing companies and a separate private sector company owning the track, signalling and stations. We have seen in chapters 13 and 14 that this was the most fiercely contested and most costly transport legislation of the twentieth century.

In chapters 7 and 9 the reader was reminded that the Ministry of Transport Act of 1919 and the Transport Act of 1947 were of a different character. Although the Act of 1919 was a pale shadow of Sir Eric (later Lord) Geddes' original, far more comprehensive Bill; under Section 3(b) the Minister of Transport was empowered after giving one month's notice to parties concerned, 'to take possession of the whole or any part of any railway undertaking, light railway or canal'.[1] This plan for the new ministry to control and, if judged expedient, to own, all the principal means of transport was rendered nugatory by the influence of the road lobby and the transformation of a department, intended to be all-embracing in its scope, to one pre-occupied with roads and motor vehicles. The measure which came nearest to success was the Attlee government's Transport Act of 1947. The understanding of Herbert Morrison, who was the 'power behind the throne' but not actually the Minister of Transport, was that the legislation had to be comprehensive in its coverage. In 1953 the BTC's Road Haulage Executive was hived off not because the Commission was unsuccessful – though it had its short-comings– but because publicly owned haulage was showing signs of being too successful.

The lesson taught by these events is that an overall view of transport is needed and that legislation dealing with all the main aspects of it should be passed in the next parliament. It is agreed that the state of the national health service and of the schools is in urgent need of rectification and that the restoration of full employment must be a priority. But there is no valid reason for arguing that an incoming Labour government could not spare the time for drastic, but carefully considered, action to revive public transport on rail and road. Nor can it be convincingly maintained that the nation could not afford it. It could. The Attlee government's financial position in 1945-7 was decidedly weaker than would be that of a Labour government in 1997. After a very destructive and costly war, lasting six years, the

UK's finances were on a 'knife's edge', especially after the sudden ending in August 1945 of American Lend-Lease which had helped to feed British people (dehydrated food saved shipping space), and the physical damage and severe wear and tear sustained by the railways. In spite of this the Labour government found the means and time to pass the Education Act, the National Health Service Act and legislation to nationalise the Bank of England, Coal mining, electricity and transport in the short space of two sessions in 1946 and 1947. In some respects the times were more favourable to the introduction of public ownership of railways and road passenger services and freight traffic in 1947 than they were fifty years later. At the end of World War II there were less than two million private cars on Britain's roads and just over half a million motor trucks.[2] People were accustomed to travelling by train, passenger journeys made being more numerous than at any time since 1927. The Labour Party under Clement Attlee's leadership received a clear electoral mandate to establish 'public ownership of inland transport'. A big difference near the close of 1996 was that there were more than twenty times as many private cars on the roads as there had been fifty years earlier, causing many millions of, but not all, car owners to be only slightly aware, or completely unaware, of the need for a better railway.

Financially, however, the nation is better placed for the transition to public ownership than it was in 1947. The fixed assets of BR, in the form of track, stations, signalling and property were sold off as Railtrack in May 1996 at less than one third of the auditor's valuation of them a few months earlier.[3] Thus, if Railtrack was bought back at the price which had been paid for it – under two billion pounds – the revenue from passengers on the parts of the network still owned by BR and the access charges paid by the 17 companies to whom franchises had been sold, would be more than adequate to pay off the interest and capital on any loan made by the European Investment Bank or by the Treasury. The Attlee government in 1947 overvalued the assets of the four main line rail-ways taken over and in so doing placed a millstone of higher interest rates round the neck of the BTC and its successors until 1988. No future Labour government should fall into this kind of trap. Since those Tories still supporting private ownership will argue that advocating a return to public ownership is merely following the old dogma of 'nationalisation'– an argument that ill befits the champion dogmatists in government this century– it is worth setting out the reasons for re-establishing a unified, publicly owned, railway system.

When passengers enquire about the route to take to their destination and the types of ticket available, the booking clerk should be the employee of BR and not someone working for a privately owned ROC with a vested interest in securing the use of one line and one type of ticket to the exclusion of an alternative possibly more beneficial to the traveller.

There should be one national time table. In 1995 in the absence of an overriding authority – BR – responsible for its compilation three attempts were needed so secure such a volume, the first two being completely unsatisfactory.

That is not the only service for which a central body is responsible. Before privatisation BR maintained a rodent pest removal service. From their central depot the mousers were sent to locations where they were most urgently needed. After the Railways Act 1993 came into operation, BR, Railtrack and the ROCs could not agree on the responsibility for and the location of these public servants. One can imagine the strain on the cats, not knowing where their next home would be and where their next meal of mice would come from!

More seriously, an overall view is required to determine priorities for investment in the railway and this can only be reliably taken if there is a central statistical body gathering and processing the relevant information. Such facts are also collated by the International Union of Railways which publishes data about railway performances in 36 countries, facts invaluable for comparing the performance of different railway system.[5]

A great advantage which results from public ownership of a unified railway system is that economies of scale can be obtained from the fact that the organisation is in a position to place large orders with the railway industry, reducing unit costs. The ROCs after privatisation, by contrast, had relatively small networks and each had a relatively small number of locomotives and passenger carriages. Furthermore the length of lease of most of them – the rail link to Gatwick being an exception – was limited to seven years. ROC managers have to provide dividends to their shareholders. They have a short term perspective. This predisposes them to accept offers from ROSCOs for second-hand, refurbished, rolling stock with a life span of only 15 years compared with new stock which has twice the life span and costs four times as much as the second hand variety. Mr Stig Svard, the chief executive officer of ABB Daimler Benz Transportation (Adtranz), described his proposal to convert 2000 ageing commuter trains as 'the half life quarter cost solution'.[6] When, as is needed, ROCs are brought back into public ownership it is hoped that BR will have a longer term outlook and opt for the new rolling stock which, after proper testing, has a longer lifespan and is less liable to breakdowns.

On returning British railways to the ownership by the state a future Labour government would be bringing practice in the UK broadly in line with the situation on the continent of Europe. In France with the termination of M. Mitterrand's presidency and his succession by M. Chirac, accompanied by M. Juppé as Premier in 1995, there was a political swing to the right and a demand for economies in government expenditure. An all out strike of the railway workers (les Cheminots) in December 1995 resisted the proposed 'reforms' on SNCF and resulted in an agreed compromise in June 1996. The French government took control of the infrastructure from SNCF and wiped out a large part of the debt incurred in building the TGV but left the SNCF sole responsibility for organising and running the train services. The state leased the infrastructure to SNCF which paid the 'rent', from its passenger and freight resources,[7] and was given additional funds for introducing 'green' trains and providing better information services. In contrast with the situation in the UK, it was a clear and viable arrangement. The Netherlands Railways, after early success of Rail 21 switching traffic from road to rail and reducing many fares, underwent financial difficulties in the mid 1990s but remained firmly a unified state organisation. The Belgian Railways (BDZ) and German Federal

Railways (DB) were subject to some greater commercialisation but remained under unified public control. In Sweden there was introduced in 1988 the separation of the infrastructure under the National Rail Administration, Banverket, from the running of freight and passenger trains which was thrown open to competition. However SJ, the state owned railway, was allowed to bid in opposition to private companies and won contracts to run over 90 per cent of the services. Regional transport bodies were given more say in the provision of services within their areas.[8] The general picture in Europe was of the value of unified national control, but of a greater degree of commercialism in operation.

An incoming Labour government should give priority to restoring public ownership of railways since one of the objectives is to induce the switch of transport from road to rail. If this is to take place railway passenger services and freight movement should be made more attractive so that car drivers and freight operators will find it more advantageous to use public transport.

The legislation should include provision for BR's repossession of Railtrack at the price investors paid for it in May 1996. The government should 'shop around' for a loan from the Treasury or the European Investment Bank on the best possible terms. Since Railtrack achieved operating profits of £305 m on a turnover of £2,275 m in the financial year to 31 March 1995, and also made an external financing contribution of £316 m, very favourable terms for a loan should be obtained. The government should buy up for BR the ROSCOs so that orders could quickly be placed for new rolling stock. This move should be seen as providing a demand for labour in the railway industry, and should be publicised as such. To finance the return of the ROCs to BR ownership an incoming Labour government should follow the advice given by Kenneth Clarke, the Chancellor of the Exchequer, to Michael Portillo, Secretary of State for Defence, in July 1996. He said he should
cut the defence procurement budget by 'hundreds of millions of pounds'.

If the cost of the Trident missile submarine was not included in this programme of cuts his successor could go one better than his political opposite number, by including it. This would be a far more beneficial use of taxpayers money.

In co-operation with local authorities an urgent campaign should be set on foot to reopen disused rail freight depots to provide facilities for the transference of freight from HGV on roads to rail. There would also be need to provide fiscal incentives for the owners of the vehicles making the longer distance trips by road to transfer to rail.

In 1995 the Department of Transport spent just £69,000, on researching transport by rail compared with an expenditure of £33,800,000 on road transport research. This gross imbalance of directed resources would have to be corrected.[9]

As has been shown in earlier chapters, railway fares in the UK are among the highest in Europe. A well advertised policy (nationally and locally) of lower railway fares should be adopted as the positive policy of attracting passenger traffic from road to rail

When propounding the above policies it will be necessary to point out the costs of continuing with the present policies of free enterprise drift. Cost Benefit Analysis (COBA) should include the costs of congestion and pollution. In 1989 the CBI estimated the national cost of congestion to be £15 billion.[10] By June 1996 this estimate had risen to £20 billion.[11]

It has been a fallacious assumption that taxpayers are invariably opposed to 'tax and spend' policies. Opinion polls revealed that when the Tories took office in 1979 the majority against 'tax and spend' had climbed to 2-1. But since the effects of Tory taxation policies and cuts in the welfare state have been experienced, opinions have changed. In 1992 52 per cent chose the higher taxes option. Even in the general election of that year 18.4 million of the electorate voted for parties more committed to spending on public services compared with 14 million who voted for the Tories. The policies recommended above will have to be set forth with conviction and with the explanation that their non-adoption will be more costly in the long run.[12]

Chapter Fifteen: **Notes**

1. Ministry of Transport Act, 9 and 10 George V chap. 15 August 1919.
2. Transport Statistics Great Britain, 1964-74, (1976), p.62.
3. British Railways Board, Annual Report and Accounts 1994-95, p.59 gives the gross book value of its tangible assets as at 1 April 1994 as £6,464 million. Railtrack's first Annual Report for 1994-95 p.44 gives the value of the tangible fixed assets at 31 March 1995 as £6,207.2 million, but after allowing £1,923.5 million for Accumulated depreciation puts the Net Book Value at £4,283.7 million.
4. For one of many examples of this see the chapter 'So you want to go to Bury St.Edmunds' in C.Wolmar, The Great British Railway Disaster, (1996), p.38.
5. For example, International Union of Railways, Supplementary Statistics for 1990 and 1991. Paris (1992).
6. Financial Times, 3 July 1996.
7. Temps, réel, 12 June 1996. Le Monde (editorial), 12 June 1996. SNCF, Department Communication Interne, Informations Express, 11 June 1996. Liberation, June 1996, 'Sur la voie des British Railways' an article comparing the situation in Britain and France. I am grateful to Marc Nussbaumer for this information.
8. I am grateful to Ola Johansson for this information.
9. Natural World, (The Wildlife Trust) (Spring/Summer 1996), p.11.
10. CBI Trade Routes to the Future, (1989), p.9.
11. House of Commons, Transport Committee, Session 1995/96 Third Report, 19 June 1996, Risk Reduction for Vulnerable Road Users. Memorandum from the CBI.
12. Observer, 7 July 1996 Business supplement, 'Blair's tax fears could be mistaken'.

Chapter Sixteen
Future Policy
(b) Roads

On 17 July 1996 the delegates attending the intergovernmental conference on climate change in Geneva were surprised to hear Timothy Wirth, the United States representative, align his government with those warning that there had been an alarming increase in 'greenhouse' warming of the atmosphere. J. Selwyn Gummer, the UK government's Secretary of State for the Environment, put forward a seven point plan for cutting carbon dioxide and other poisonous emissions in the industrial world. Although there was dissent from the fossil-fuel lobby in the USA and in oil and coal producing countries, there is no doubt that the majority of delegates expressed a growing concern that there should be action to reduce the emission of greenhouse gases.[1]

In 1994 the Royal Commission on Environmental Pollution found that in the second half of the twentieth century 24 per cent of carbon dioxide emissions produced in the UK came from transport and that road transport accounted for 87 per cent of transport-related emissions. It estimated that carbon dioxide emissions from road transport almost doubled between 1970 and 1990. By contrast, emissions from rail and coastal shipping had not increased significantly. It was also predicted that the further doubling of the amount of carbon dioxide in the atmosphere would increase global mean surface temperatures by between 1.5 and 4.5°C.[2]

The implication of these findings is that everything possible should be done to promote 'cleaner' cars, lorries and buses and to effect a change from environmentally 'unfriendly' to 'friendly' means of transport. This involves persuading people to change from using the car to travelling by bicycle, wherever that is feasible, and, since carbon-dioxide emissions from aircraft are substantial and growing, encouraging a switch from air travel to travel by rail or by sea.

To discourage car use there should be a change from taxing car ownership to taxing car use. Since the more the motorist uses the car the greater is the pollution of the atmosphere, the tax on petrol and diesel fuel should be increased while the licence duty should be decreased. This policy has been adopted in the Netherlands with the result that although there are more cars per head of population in that country than is the case in the UK, lower mileages per person are recorded. If petrol and diesel duties were raised by 10 per cent a year, as recommended by the transport journalist Polly Ghazi, it would encourage the car owner to make fewer trips, which would reduce road congestion and pollution and result in greater use of public transport.[3]

There remain many people who live in isolated districts not served by buses who depend entirely on their car for shopping, visiting the doctor's surgery and keeping in touch with their friends. Parallel with the increases in fuel duty local authorities would be required to provide village buses which would visit each country area at least twice a day. Bus operators would be allowed fuel duty rebates based on the degree to which their buses were new and 'green', i.e. as nearly as possible pollution free. Government grants to local authorities which have been severely cut in recent years would need to be increased to make these changes possible.

Under the Observer Blueprint for a National Travel Plan there would be variable road taxes depending on the type of vehicle used, gas-guzzling cars paying more than those with a clean technology. Under this plan many owners of vehicles would be paying less than half the standard £135 vehicle duty now paid, though they would pay more for petrol the more they used the car. The roads would be less congested and the air cleaner. When Chancellor Lawson abolished the purchase tax on new vehicles in 1992 car numbers increased. Under the Observer plan the tax would be re-introduced, but at a variable rate which would encourage the use of greener vehicles. It is estimated that these new fiscal measures would bring the Treasury £4.7 billion a year which should be earmarked to improve public transport services.

In morning and evening rush hours roads in the major conurbations are crowded with a high proportion of company cars. Free car parking at the work place can bring substantial financial gain to the company car owner, gains estimated at

£5 000 a year for those employed in city centres. Employers should be offered every incentive to give their employees such perks as rail season tickets and travelcards as substitutes for the company car. These should be tax free.

A problem of road transport that has to be tackled urgently is that of congestion. The Thatcher government's White Paper Roads for Prosperity was published in 1989. Its emphasis on road widening schemes to accommodate the extra traffic was based on the belief that this would ensure the freer movement of vehicles. Although it was admitted that there was little scope for this programme in inner cities it was claimed that, even here, traffic flows could be speeded up. This was not, in fact, achieved. There was no appreciable increase in the speed of traffic movement in central London between 1920 and 1990. The policy of 'predict and provide' embodied in the policies of the 1989 White Paper only resulted in extending the areas of congestion. A study conducted under the auspices of Friends of the Earth by D.P. McLaren and R. Higman in 1993 examined congestion in 29 national traffic census points and found that in 14 of them traffic was congested in 1990 and that if traffic growth continued at the 1993 rate, the situation would have worsened considerably so that by 2025 there would be congestion at all but one of the points.[5] The Green movement advocates a change in individual and family lifestyles as an approach which will lead to less dependence on motorised transport and therefore less road congestion and all its attendant evils. Freiburg, Delft and York are cities which have so organised communal living that between a half and a third of the journeys not made on foot are made by cycle (compared with less than 3 per cent in the UK as a whole).[6] However, not all cities are topographically or otherwise as suited to the greening of traffic as are the three abovementioned cases, and not all families in the large conurbations are so able to approach the ideal of self-sufficiency as are some village or suburban idealists. For the large majority of the population the solution must be a great improvement in public transport.

Electrically powered public transport in the form of light railways or tramways occupy less land, can carry large concentrations of passengers and at the same time be more energy efficient than private cars. In 1994 the Royal Commission found that

it is clear that present use of rail transport in the UK is significantly more energy efficient than the present use of road transport, and that use of water to move freight is considerably more energy efficient than other modes.

It also found that bus and coach travel is 'significantly more efficient than travel by private car'.[7]

The main solution to the road congestion and pollution problem is to secure a switch from private car use to energy-efficient forms of public transport.

To effect this change a reorganisation of the Department of Transport is needed. A new National Public Transport Agency within the Department would be allocated the task of improving air quality, reducing traffic growth, inducing travellers to switch from cars to public transport, walking or cycling, and cutting carbon dioxide emissions and noise levels from vehicles.[8]

Before the passing of the Transport Act 1985 most of Britain's buses were publicly owned. They either belonged to the National Bus Company or municipalities. Arguing that privatisation was needed to increase competition and the stimulus to efficiency which followed, the NBC was split into 72 separate companies. In the 1990s a merger movement which has gathered momentum in most recent months has resulted in three companies – FirstBus, Stagecoach and Cowie – gaining control of over 50 per cent of the market share. See Fig.12. The three next largest companies control a further 20 per cent of the market.[9] Thus, a decade after deregulation it is becoming apparent that a publicly owned and controlled industry has given place to one privately owned and increasingly out of control. Furthermore some of the bus companies were being granted franchises as ROCs. Stagecoach acquired South West Trains in 1995 and the coach company National Express has acquired two passenger rail franchises one of which, the Midland Main Line, runs services between Leeds, Derby, Nottingham and London (St.Pancras) parallel with its coach route between the same cities. The Office of Fair Trading (OFT) has urged National

Express to drop its coach services between Nottingham and London and to encourage new competitors to enter the market. National Express has not, so far, complied.[10]

FIG.12   Market share of British Bus operators.

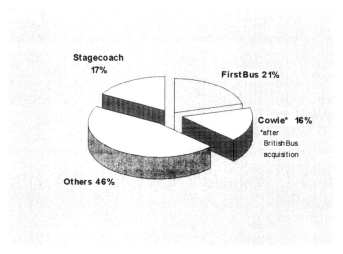

Source: The Guardian, June 19 1996.

Clare Short, then the Labour Party's front bench spokeswoman on transport, told the RMT's bus workers' grade conference in London that

it was not Labour's intention to buy a load of clapped-out old buses.[11]

But if the momentum of take-overs continues and the giant bus companies continue their monopolistic practices, defy the warnings of the OFT and pay scant regard to the human needs of their employees in respect of working conditions and excessive hours, the restoration of public ownership of the bus industry at local or national level may prove necessary.

There is a widespread impression that heavy lorries, though they obstruct the view of other road users, have a better safety record than private cars. In fact fatal casualty rates, aggregated over all classes of road, are 2.4 times higher for lorries than for cars, and this is remarkable as a larger proportion of lorry travel than of car travel takes place on motorways which have lower accident rates than other roads. The conclusion of the Civic Trust is that

in any driving situation, lorries pose a greater threat than cars to the safety of road users.[12]

It is black smoke (particulates) which is the most objectionable form of pollution caused by heavy lorries. It soils buildings and is an aggravating factor in respiratory diseases.

In 1990 the Building Research Establishment found, in a sample survey, that most people questioned found that the noise of road traffic bothered them more than noise from aircraft, trains or neighbours, although of course it varied greatly from location to location.[13]

The physical damage caused by heavy lorries may well be the costliest, in financial terms, of all the damage they do to the environment. It is an everyday experience of the pedestrian to see pavement bollards, street signs, street lamps and curbside metal fencing knocked down by such vehicles. It is easy to attribute these mishaps to the carelessness of lorry drivers when the truth is that the HGVs from which they deliver goods are unsuited to the relatively narrow roads in which they have to operate.

In the light of the environmental damage caused by HGVs it is highly desirable that, where feasible, freight traffic should be diverted from road to rail or inland or coastal waterways. To achieve this objective a change in the present taxation system will be needed. The taxes currently paid include vehicle excise duty VAT on purchase both of the main item and any spare parts needed and fuel tax. The excise duty, which is usually paid annually, is levied however much or little the vehicle is used. Instead, as is proposed above for cars, the excise duty should be lowered simply as a means of financing the Driver and Vehicle Licensing Centre at Swansea, but that fuel duty, especially on diesel and derv, should be increased. In addition there should be an environmental tax per kilometre travelled based on the weight on each axle when the lorry is fully loaded, the number of axles and the space the stationery vehicle occupies. These measures should be combined with the opening up of old and new railway sidings, and depots, advocated in chapter 15, and a bonus for operators who switch their vehicles to rail or coastal vessel for at least a part of the journey.

On Wednesday July 10 1996 Sir George Young, the Secretary of State for Transport, launched the National Cycling Strategy to encourage and make less hazardous, cycling to work and for pleasure. A National Cycling Forum chaired by the local transport minister is to be established to sponsor local authority cooperation and to report annually on progress made. £10 million was set aside to finance these plans. Such an initiative was long overdue. The vehicle kilometres covered by cyclists in Britain in 1996 at 4.5 billion – was little more than one sixth of the distance covered in 1946. Britain lags well behind her European partners. In the UK slightly less than two per cent of all trips made were by cycle whereas in Sweden one in ten trips were by this means, a figure slightly exceeded by Germany and well beaten by Denmark which notched up eighteen per cent.[14] Since the early 1980s Sustrans, which stands for Sustainable Transport, has been trying to build up a national cycle network, believing that many more people would choose to make shorter journeys by cycle – if road conditions were amenable. The Corporation of the City of London in collaboration with the Royal Borough of Kingston on Thames publicised the London Cycle Network which was a plan to develop over 2,000 kilometres of local cycle routes throughout the capital.[15] It was expected to cost about £50 million which would be raised by the DoT, the London boroughs, the City Corporation and the Millennium Fund. Progress so far has been patchy, but in the Borough of Hackney recently a cycle route was painted green on the roads. Other pioneers have been the cities of York and Peterborough and the Forest of Dean District Council which, in alliance with Forest Enterprise, is using old canal towpaths and disused railways to create off-road family cycling.[16] It is to be hoped that other local authorities will follow these excellent examples and that the government in Westminster will restore the level of support to local authorities to make it possible.

It is not a question of local authorities embarking on a big spending spree. It is a matter of showing foresightedness rather

178

than shortsightedness. The UK Cyclists Public Affairs Group told the Commons Select Committee on Transport that, with the German level of cycle use – 11 per cent of trips – the saving amounted to £1 billion each year, comprising £700 million in congestion cost savings; £130 million in pollution cost savings and £200 million in benefits to health.[17]

That there could be some conflict of interest between walkers and cyclists was pointed out to the same Transport Committee by the Ramblers Association witness, representing 100,000 members. Just as the cyclists' representative had argued the case for a National Cycle Network the Pedestrian Association pleaded for

a network of safe and convenient routes for walkers in
town and countryside alike

and went on to stress the

need for any increased provision for cyclists, whether via
the proposed National Cycle-Network or otherwise, not to
increase the risk to walkers or to be perceived to do so.[18]

Clearly it will be the duty of any incoming government to see that there is adequate, safe, provision for cyclists – and motor cyclists which pollute the atmosphere less than buses.

Chapter Sixteen: Notes

1. The Guardian, 18 July 1996.
2. Royal Commission on Environmental Pollution, 18th Report, Transport and the Environment, (1994), pp.40-41.
3. Polly Ghazi, 'Use taxes to make Britain's roads safer, cleaner and less crowded', in The Observer, Blueprint for a National Travel Plan to take Britain's Transport System into the 21st Century, (1995), p.4.
4. Ibid.
5. D.P. McLaren and R. Higman, The environmental implications on the interuban network in the UK (1993). Financial Times, 3 March 1996.
6. Transport and the Environment, (1994), p.89.
7. Ibid., p.91.
8. Observer Blueprint, p.4.
9. Geoff Dyer, 'Carve up on the buses' in Financial Times, Weekend

Money, July 13/14 1996.
10. Financial Times, 16 July 1996.
11. RMT News, July 1996, p.12.
12. S. Plowden and Keith Buchan (for the Civic Trust), A new framework for freight transport, (1995), p.51.
13. Ibid., pp.54-55.
14. The Guardian, 11 July 1996.
15. London Cycle Network Steering Group, This is the London Cycle Network.
16. Forest of Dean Newspapers, 7 June 1996, p.13.
17. Commons Transport Committee, Session 1995-6, Third Report, 19 June 1996, Risk Reduction for Vulnerable Road Users. II 8.
18. Ibid., p.59.

180

Chapter Seventeen
Future Policy
(c) Water and Air Transport

There has been a sad decline in the use made of Britain's canals since the Beeching era though in the last quarter of the century the fall in the volume of goods lifted has not been as dramatic as it was in the third quarter. Between 1983 and 1993 the freight lifted fell quite sharply from 9 to 6 million tonnes; but this was offset by the more gentle decline in the volume of work done, measured in tonne-kilometres. Here the fall was of some eight per cent, from 2.4 to 2.2 billion tonne kilometre (btk).[1] A map included in the Transport Department's statistics for 1995 shows twelve major waterways in the United Kingdom. These were the Thames; the Medway; Severn; Mersey; the Manchester Ship Canal; Clyde; Forth; Humber; Ouse, Aire and Calder Navigation; the Trent and the Orwell.[2] Measured in terms of freight moved, the Thames took the lion's share in 1989 with 0.15 btk, with the Humber coming second with 0.04 btk. What was remarkable was the decline of Thames traffic in the years 1989-93 by more than half, due to the falling off in the carriage of coal and coke for gasworks.[3]

In the 1980s and 1990s the renovation of important canal routes was left to the initiative of local groups mobilising the support of county councils and the Department of the Environment. In 1986 the Rochdale Canal was threatened by a road scheme. The DoE backed the local enthusiasts by ordering a public enquiry which ruled in favour of the canal preservationists. Then, in March 1996, the canal won an £11.9 million lottery award. In the same month Audrey Smith, chair of the Inland Waterways Association, wrote to John Major appealing for his intervention to save the Thames and Severn Canal which was threatened with bisection because of a private road development. Although the activists had been working for 20 years to save the entire canal and although the Gloucestershire County Council was supportive, it is still in doubt whether the plan for a navigable culvert under the road will receive the necessary financial backing.[4]

The Departments of Transport and the Environment are agreed in envisaging the future of the canals mainly as centres for leisure activity. There is no conception of their playing any major part in easing the volume of traffic on Britain's roads. Simon Salem, the marketing and communications manager of the British Waterways Board, expressed the consensus view when he declared:

We have to appreciate that many people enjoy going onto the canals to gongoozle — to simply watch the wildlife and canal life go by. Our aim is to increase everybody's enjoyment of this natural resource.

However, both the DoE and the Waterways Board want to increase the Board's revenue. In 1994 its earnings amounted to 40 per cent of its annual running costs of £87 million and 25 per cent of its earnings came from leisure receipts. The opening up of tea-shops, small museums and playgrounds are seen as the principal means of improving the financial position.[5]

There is scope for an incoming government to plan for the more extensive use of Britain's inland waterways for the movement of freight. An examination of the record of our EU partners shows that they made far better use of transport by inland waterways than did the UK. It is true that Germany had the enormous advantage of the river Rhine, but even so, its movement of freight increased from 51.7 btk in 1982 to 57.1 btk in 1992. The Netherlands have historically made very good use of canals; nevertheless government policies secured an increase of traffic from 30.8 btk to 35.7 btk over the same decade. Although in France there was a fall of just under 20 per cent in traffic moved, it was still in 1992 43 times as much as was achieved in Britain.[6] Just as a specially mobilised workforce is recommended to reopen rail freight depots, another is advocated to open up vital inland waterways links.

It is little appreciated how diverse is the coastal trade of the UK. A recent survey by Bernard McCall recorded 149 ports in the UK as far apart as Newlyn, Ramsgate, Wick, and Briton Ferry. They ranged from the smallest havens where coasters put in only two or three times a year to Blyth which in 1961 was the biggest coal handling port in Europe, exporting nearly 7 million tons annually. Although fossil fuels and ferrous metals in the early part of the present century ensured that coasters carried a greater ton-mileage than did the railways, the cargoes carried are now more diversified. Bulk commodities carried relatively long distances, such as dredged sand, timber, scrap iron and fertilizers, still predominate. Other commodities traded include concrete blocks (sent to Lundy Island from Yelland), petroleum products, sprats from Torbay, animal feedstuffs, sugar beet, grain and many more.

Most of the coastal trade is in the hands of small firms with tiny fleets of ships. An exception is the still largely family owned company of Everard, founded in 1880 by a foreman shipwright at Greenhithe. Its dry cargo fleet in 1992 comprised 18 vessels ranging from 3000 to 5000 tons displacement. The latest vessel in the fleet is the Motor Vessel Seniority of 5,163 tons built at Appledore in Devon. To enable the ship to maximise the cargoes carried to ports with draft and tidal restrictions it was designed with a shallow draft and is able to load and discharge cargo aground.[7]

In the last quarter century new technologies in ship design such as those embodied in the Seniority mentioned above, have aided the survival of Britain's coastal trade. These innovations include hydraulic wheelhouses which can be raised or lowered to enable boats to pass under low-arched bridges; collapsible masts which serve the same purpose and bow ramps to enable ships to take aboard ro-ro (roll on – roll off) cargoes.

It will always be an important role of coastal transport to maintain passenger and cargo links between the UK mainland and the islands of the British Isles. The ro-ro ferries linking Southampton and Cowes, Portsmouth and Ryde are vital links between the mainland and the Isle of Wight. This is also true of services to the Isle of Man, the Channel Islands and the Orkney, Shetland and Western Isles of Scotland.

In his Foreword to the government's response to the transport debate Transport: the Way Forward, Sir George Young, the Secretary of State for Transport, notes that there has been much discussion on the roles of road and rail in the provision of transport, but admits that 'shipping issues' are not covered in depth in this large format 138 page report.[8] This is an indication of a missed opportunity which should be rectified by an incoming government.

As has been shown in chapter 5 domestic air passenger flights in the UK represented less than a quarter of aircraft movements at UK airports.[9] By contrast the number of passengers on international scheduled services to and from the UK between 1982 and 1992 more than doubled. About two thirds of these international flights were for tourism.[10] International flights from Heathrow, Gatwick and, to a lesser extent, Manchester had so increased that there were vociferous demands for an additional runway at Heathrow. The Commons Select Committee on Transport made Airport Capacity the subject of its second report of the 1995-96 session published in July 1996. Before it, was, among others, a memorandum from the Air Transport Users' Council which advocated that

> measures identified by the Heathrow Airport Runway
> Capacity Enhancement Study for increasing throughput
> at Heathrow should be introduced as soon as possible.[11]

This view was contested by witnesses from the Council for the Preservation of Rural England (CPRE) who had received hundreds of reports from their members in the South East of the disturbance to country life by the noise of aircraft and the pollution air flight caused to the atmosphere. They were aware that the Royal Commission in 1994 had reported that

> aircraft are noisier than other forms of transport, and
> noise is the most intrusive aspect of air transport.[12]

They were also aware that emissions of pollutants and greenhouse gases from aircraft were proportionately greater at low flight levels, at take-off and taxi-ing, than at higher levels and on longer flights.[13]

The CPRE's memorandum therefore included the statement:

> We believe that the government needs to see air travel
> as a component of an integrated transport policy.[14]

Furthermore, they advocated

> Differential pricing mechanisms ... to ensure the cost of
> air travel better reflects its full economic and environ-
> mental effects compared with other transport modes

and considered that there needed to be

> an investment in rail links between regional airports so
> as to facilitate the sharing of current resources and
> encourage interchange facilities to allow easier access
> from air to rail.[15]

In its representative's evidence the Department of Transport advocated the distribution of air traffic to the less fully used airports, but said little about rail alternatives to air transport.

The evidence given to the Select Committee and its Report to the mind of the author of this book suggests the need for a reformed Department of Transport, better equipped to implement policies which have taken full account of the different transport modes. A department so changed might well advocate fiscal measures to encourage a switch of internationally bound passengers from air to Eurostar and the Channel Tunnel and links to the European rail network as desirable on economic and environmental grounds.

On 22 July 1996 the Civil Aviation Authority announced that

> it was delegating safety issues to airlines and airports
> to minimise the regulatory burden on the industry.

The Authority denied that it was increasing the risk to air travellers. It said the change

> would allow the Authority to concentrate on auditing
> airlines 'safety systems rather than being involved in
> prescriptive inspection proceedures'.[16]

However, just three days later it was revealed for the first time to the media, that a British Midlands Boeing 737, bound for Lanzarote from Luton airport in February 1995, was forced to return to its base in an emergency landing within eleven minutes of take-off, due to a severe leak of oil. A fitter had failed to replace engine covers. There was no proper check up and ground level testing of the aircraft before departure. Only the very prompt action of the pilot and crew saved them and the 183 passengers from the major catastrophe of an uncontrolled landing.[17] It would appear there was something to be said for those 'prescriptive inspection procedures' carried out by an independent authority after all.

Chapter Seventeen: **Notes**

1. Transport Statistics Great Britain, 1994, (1995), Sect. 6.9, p.138.
2. Transport Statistics Great Britain, 1995, (1996), Sect. 6.10, p.139.
3. Ibid., Section 6.11, p.140.
4. The Guardian, 23 April 1996.
5. Financial Times, 25 May 1994.
6. Transport Statistics Great Britain, 1994, (1995), Table 8.5, p.171.
7. Information pack on the firm of Everard kindly lent by Professor John Armstrong.
8. Transport: the Way Forward. The Government's response to the Transport Debate (April 1996), p.5.
9. A fact confirmed by the Royal Commission on Environmental Pollution, (1994), p.63.
10. Ibid.
11. Commons Select Committee on Transport, Session 1995-6, 2nd Report, UK Airport Capacity, vol.2, pp.39-40.
12. Royal Commission on Environmental Pollution: Aircraft noise p.66.
13. Ibid., p.68.
14. Ibid.
15. UK Airport Capacity, vol.2, p.95.
16. Financial Times, 23 July 1996.
17. The Guardian, 26 July 1996.

186

Abbreviations used in the text

AA	Automobile Association
ASLEF	Associated Society of Locomotive Engineers and Firemen
ASRS	Amalgamated Society of Railway Servants
BDZ	Belgian Railways (see also: SNCB)
BEA	British European Airways
BOAC	British Overseas Airways Corporation
BR	British Railways
BRB	British Railways Board
BRF	British Road Federation
BRS	British Road Services
BTC	British Transport Commission
btk	billion tonne kilometre
BUA	British United Airways
CBI	Confederation of British Industry
CER	Community of European Railways
COBA	Cost Benefit Analysis
CPRE	Council for the Preservation of Rural England
CTCC	Central Transport Consultative Committee
CTRL	Channel Tunnel Rail Link
DoE	Department of the Environment
DoT	Department of Transport
EFL	External Financing Limit
GDP	Gross Domestic Product
GNP	Gross National Product
GWR	Great Western Railway
HSE	Health and Safety Executive
HGVs	Heavy Goods Vehicles
HMSO	Her Majesty's Stationery Office
ICE	Institution of Civil Engineers
ICI	Imperial Chemical Industries
LCC	London County Council
LNER	London and North Eastern Railway
LMS	London, Midland and Scottish Railway
MLC	Motor Legislation Committee
NBC	National Bus Company
NER	North Eastern Railway
NHS	National Health Service
NUR	National Union of Railwaymen
OECD	Organisation for Economic Co-operation and Development
OFT	Office of Fair Trading

187

Opraf	Office of Rail Franchising
PSO	Public Service Obligation
PSV	Public Service Vehicle
PTA	Passenger Transport Authorities
RAC	Royal Automobile Club
RAS	Railway Air Services
RCA	Railway Companies' Association
REC	Railway Executive Committee
RHA	Road Haulage Association
RHE	Road Haulage Executive
RIA	Roads Improvement Association
RMT	Rail, Maritime and Transport Workers Union
ROCs	Rail Operating Companies
ROSCOs	Rolling Stock Companies
SMMT	Society of Motor Manufacturers and Traders
SNCF	Société nationale des Chemins de fer français
TGV	Train à la Grande Vitesse
TGWU	Transport and General Workers Union
TOC	Train Operating Company
TOUs	Train Operating Units
TSSA	Transport Salaried Staffs' Association
TUC	Trades Union Congress

Select Bibliography

R. Adley, Out of Steam (1990).
D. Aldcroft, British Railways in Transition (1968).
G. Alderman, The Railway Interest (1973).
J. Armstrong, Railways and Coastal Shipping in Britain in the Later Nineteenth Century: Cooperation and Competition in C. Wrigley and J. Shepherd On the Move (1991).
P.S. Bagwell, The Transport Revolution 1770-1985 (2nd Edn. 1988).
T.C. Barker and M. Robbins, A History of London Transport, vol.2 (1974).
M.R. Bonavia, British Rail, the first 25 years (1981),
British Railway Policy between the Wars (1981).
B. Castle, The Castle Diaries 1964-70 (1984), and Fighting all the Way (1993).

T. Coppack, A Lifetime with Ships: the Autobiography of a Coasting
Shipowner (1973).
J.S. Dodson, Bus deregulation and Privatisation (1988).
R.S. Doganis, A National Airport Plan (1967, Fabian Tract 377).
H.J. Dyos and D.H. Aldcroft, British Transport. An Economic Survey from
the Seventeenth Century to the Twentieth (1969).
C.D. Foster, The Transport Problem (1963).
Friends of the Earth, Guide to Traffic Calming in Residential Areas (1987).
D.D. Gladwin, The Canals of Britain (1973), and The Waterways of
Britain (1978).
T.R. Gourvish, British Railways 1948-73, A Business History (1986).
K. Grieves, Sir Eric Geddes (1989).
H. Gripaios, Tramp Shipping (1959).
M. Hamer, Wheels within Wheels (1987).
J. Hibbs, The History of British Bus Services (1968).
M. Hillman and A. Whalley, The Social Consequences of Rail Closures (1980).
HMSO, Road Accidents Great Britain 1994, (1995).
Transport Statistics Great Britain (annually).
P. Jones, Public Attitudes to Transport Policy and the Environment,
Transport Studies Department, University of Westminster (1996).
W. Keegan, Mrs Thatcher's Economic Experiment (1984).
B. McCall, Coasters around Britain (1989).
D. Maltby and H.P. White, Transport in the United Kingdom (1983).
D.L. Munby and A.H. Watson, Inland Transport Statistics Great
Britain 1900-1970, (1978).
P. Parker, For Starters: the Business of Life (1989).
S. Plowden, Taming Traffic (1980).
W. Plowden, The Motor Car and Politics 1896-1970, (1971).
J.D. Porteous, Canal Ports (1977).
R. Pryke, The Rail Problem (1975).
K. Richardson, The British Motor Industry 1896-1939, (1977).
Royal Commission on Environmental Pollution, 18th Report, Transport and
the Environment (1994).
J. Simmons, The Victorian Railway (1991).
D. Starkie, The Motorway Age (1982).
M.P. R. Strohl, Europe's High Speed Trains (1994).
TEST (Transport and Environment Studies) Wrong Side of the Tracks (1991).
R. Watson and M. Gray, The Penguin Book of the Bicycle (1978).
S. Wheatcroft, Air Transport Policy (1964).
J. Whitelegg, Transport for a sustainable future (1993).
H. Wilson, The Labour Government 1964-70. A Personal Record (1971).
W. Wolf, Car Mania (1996).
C. Wolmar, The Great British Railway Disaster (1996).
R. Worcester, Roots of British Air Policy (1966).

Chronology

1896	Locomotives on Highways Act.
1901	RAC founded.
1903-4	Motor Car Act introduced Driving Licenses.
	Speed limit 20 mph.
1905	AA founded.
1907	First Motor-race meeting at Brooklands.
1908	The first Ford Model 'T' produced in the USA.
1911	Ford opened car plant at Old Trafford, Manchester.
	First national railway strike.
1913	National Union of Railwaymen (NUR) founded.
1914-19	Railway Executive Committee set up to manage railways for the duration of war.
1919	Ministry of Transport Act.
1921	Railways Act grouped railways into four main line companies.
1925-31	Ford Motor Works moved to Dagenham.
1926	General Strike.
1927	First automatic traffic light signals installed.
1928-32	Royal Commission on Transport.
1930	Road Traffic Act. Speed limit of 20 mph abolished for cars and cycles. PSVs limited to 30 mph. Maximum working hours for PSV and goods vehicle drivers introduced. Compulsory third party insurance.
1931	Highway Code introduced.
1932	British Road Federation formed.
1934	Road Traffic Act 30 mph speed limit in built up areas.
1936	First Belisha Beacon road crossings.
1938	Railways' 'Square Deal' campaign.
1939-45	Railway Executive Committee.
	Signposts removed during wartime.
1945-48	Petrol allowance enough for 180 miles driving a month.
1947	Transport Act nationalises the principal means of transport. British Transport Commission oversees separate Executives for Railways, London Transport, Docks and Inland Waterways, Hotels and Road Transport.
1949	Road Transport Executive split into (a) Road Haulage Executive and (b) Road Passenger Executive.
1949-54	School Crossing Patrols (Lollipop men) legislation. Flashing indicators on motor vehicles legalised.
1953	Transport Act abolished the Road Haulage Executive, most of whose assets were sold.
1955	Railway Modernisation Plan.
1958	Preston by-pass opened.
1959	First stage of M1 Motorway opened.
1962	Transport Act. Dissolution of the BTC. Establishment of British Railways, London Transport, British Transport Docks and British Waterways.
1963	Beeching Report.

1964	Trial speed limit of 70 mph on Motorways.
1965	Drink and Drive publicity campaign.
1966	Seat Belts compulsory for new cars.
1966	Breathalyser Tests introduced.
1968	Transport Act. Grants for socially necessary railways. National Freight Corporation founded.
1969	First bus lanes introduced, in Park Lane, London.
1973	Safety Helmets made compulsory for two-wheeled motor vehicle users.
1975-6	Mini-roundabouts introduced.
1979	Conservative election victory. Margaret Thatcher Prime Minister. Use of tachographs accepted by government.
1980	Transport Act removed licensing restrictions from express bus services.
1981	Five week strike by merchant seamen over pay claim. Zonal system on London Underground. London Transport bus and underground fares cut by 32%. December: House of Lords rules that fare reductions financed from rates are illegal.
1982	ASLEF and NUR strikes against service cuts and pay offer.
1983	Seat Belt wearing compulsory for drivers and front seat passengers. Maximum gross weight for articulated goods vehicles raised from 32.5 tonnes to 38 tonnes. Travel cards introduced by London Underground. Wheel clamps introduced.
1984	National coal strike. BR's Sealink sold to Sea Containers.
1985	First competitive tendering for a London bus route. Transport Act. Bus deregulation.
1986	Anglo French Channel Tunnel fixed link Treaty signed. Formal enquiry into loss of M.V. Derbyshire, sunk in 1980.
1987	Privatisation of British Airways and British Airports Authority. November: Fire at King's Cross Underground. 32 Killed. Travellers' Fare privatised.
1988	Close proximity and wide angle view mirrors compulsory for HGVs. Uniform construction standards applied to minibuses. High speed river bus service opened in London. Multiple rail crash at Clapham Junction. 35 killed.
1989	Compulsory basic training for motorcyclists introduced.
1990	John Major succeeds Margaret Thatcher as Premier.
1992	April: Conservative Party re-elected with a very small majority. Traffic Calming Act. White Paper, New Opportunities for the Railways published.
1993	2 February, Second Reading of Railways Bill in Commons. 5 November, Railways Bill enacted.
1994	'Kill your Speed' campaign.
1995	Deregulation of bus services in London.
1996	20 May, sale of Railtrack shares.

Index

196

Railway Policy, (1967), 107-8
(1979) 16-7
(1983) 127
(1992) 137
Railway Staffs National Tribunal, 17
railways, see also BR
industrial relations, 14, 16, 63-4,
81, 84, 96, 112
investment, 5, 11-4, 21, 47, 50, 95-6,
121, 123, 128-9, 134-42,
148-9, 153, 156-7, 166, 184
nationalisation, see also 'N', 14, 38,
58, 60, 77-8, 80-2, 85-6, 105,
108, 129, 164, 166
pensions, 160-1
productivity, 6, 11, 14-5, 17, 50, 95,
112, 135
staff numbers, 6, 14, 16, 101, 159-60
support from public funds, 6-8, 11, 49,
64, 119, 126, 128
Ramblers Association, 178
Raymond, Sir S., 107-8
'Red flag' law, 19, 65
Reid, Sir R., 121, 130, 136, 153, 157
research, 30, 33, 146, 169, 176
Ridley, N., 124-5, 130, 136
Rifkind, M., 130-1
RMT, 154, 160, 175
road accidents, cost of, see accidents
road and rail costs, 11, 15, 17, 69
road construction costs, 9
Road Fund, 67-9, 102
Road Haulage Association, 50, 79, 105
Road Haulage Disposal Board, 87-8
Road Haulage Executive, 86, 88, 95, 164
road lobby, 4, 50, 59-61, 65, 71-73, 79,
80, 83-5, 94, 107, 114, 129, 164
road rage, 34
road signposts, 29
Road Transport Executive, 21, 86
Roads for Prosperity, (1989), 173
Roads Improvement Association, 66
Rochdale Canal, 180
rodent pest control, 166
rolling stock, 12-3, 39, 50, 96, 101,
121, 137, 149, 157-60, 167-8

ROSCOs, 167-8
Royal Commissions
Canals (1906), 3
Environmental Pollution (1995),
23-4, 174
Transport (1928-30), 69

S

safety, 28-31, 67, 141, 146, 154-6
air, 184
railway, 12-3, 50, 69, 128, 135,
139, 141, 146, 154-5, 160
road, 19, 31, 33, 50, 94, 123, 175-6
Salmon, R., 148-9, 158
Scottish Bus group (1968), 109
Sealink UK, 122
seat belts, 30
Select Committees
Nationalised Industries (1960), 99
Transport, 13, 60, 125-6, 153-5,
178, 183-4
Serpell Report (1983), 16, 127-8
Short, Clare, 152, 175
Signal Engineers, Institute of Railway,
12-13, 154
signal workers strike (1994), 17-18
Snape, P., 123, 145-6
SNCF, 8, 167
Society of Motor Manufacturers and
Traders, 65-72
Somme, 55
speed limits, 19, 30, 32, 50, 70, 114
speeding, 52, 70
Square Deal campaign, 74
Stagecoach, 158, 174
Stamp, Sir J., (later Lord Stamp), 69
Stanley, Sir A., (later Lord Ashfield),
57-59, 70
Stedeford Committee Report, 99
Stokes, Sir J., 133
street furniture, 25
Swedish railways, 13, 130, 143, 168
sweeteners, 150-3
Swift, R., 149

T

Thatcher, Baroness M., 8, 12, 16-7,
46, 49, 51-2, 140, 151, 163, 173
policy on road and rail, 119-30
and rail privatisation, 129-31, 151
Thomas, J.H., 58, 61
timetables, 52, 159, 166
Todt, Dr. F., 73
Tordoff, Lord, 145
traffic lights, 29
trains, 12, 17, 29, 59, 135, 159, 160,
167-8, 174
Eurostar, 152
freight, 11, 40
TGV, 47

Transport and General Workers
Union, 76
Transport 2000, 4
Transport Committee (Commons),
12-3, 51, 124-6, 137, 139,
153-4, 155, 178
Transport, Department of, 24, 28, 31,
32-3, 51-2, 62, 77, 107, 112,
117, 123-6, 136, 141, 143,
148, 150, 169, 174, 184
Transport of Freight, (1967), 108
Transport in London, (1968), 108
Transport and Traffic, (1967), 108
Transport Retort, 4
Trident, 168-9
TUC, 16, 76-7, 81, 124, 155

U

U boat warfare and coastal trade, 40-4

V

VE Day, 25
Vehicle Inspectorate Agency, 31

W

Walker, P., (later Lord Walker of
Worcester), 111
walkers, 178
Weighell, S., 4
Welsby, J.K., 14, 150
Wilson, B., 148
Wilson, H., (later Lord Wilson of
Riveaux), 102-3, 107-8, 110, 136

Y

Young, Sir G., 152, 177, 182
Youth Hostels Association, 2
York, 101, 158, 173, 177.

By the same author

The Railwaymen: the History of the National Union of Railwaymen,
Allen and Unwin (1963).

The Railway Clearing House in the British Economy 1842-1922,
Allen and Unwin (1968).

Industrial Relations. Government and Society in Nineteenth Century
Britain. Commentaries on British Parliamentary Papers,
General editor P. Ford, Irish University Press (1974).

The Transport Revolution from 1770, Batsford (1974). Second extended
edition, Routledge (1988).

The Railwaymen, vol.2. *The Beeching Era and After,*
Allen and Unwin (1982).

End of the Line: the Fate of British Railways under Thatcher,
Verso (1984). A Japanese translation for Kokuro, the Japanese
National Railway Workers' Union, 1985.

Outcast London: a Christian Response. The West London Mission of the
Methodist Church 1887-1987, Epworth Press (1987).

Doncaster, 1853-1990: Town of Train makers,
Wheaton (1991).

Also jointly with Professor G. E. Mingay
Britain and America: A Study of Economic Change, 1850-1939,
Routledge (1970), reprinted 1971, 1987. Japanese edition,
Japan UNI Agency (1970).

and jointly with Joan Lawley
*From Prison Cell to Council Chamber: the Life of Philip William Bagwell
1885-1958,* Sessions (1994).

Other Socialist Renewal titles

Is Socialism Inseparable from Common Ownership?
by G. A. Cohen   50p

New Directions for Pensions
How to Revitalise National Insurance
by Peter Townsend and Alan Walker   £1.50

New Labour's Aims and Values
A Study in Ambiguity
by Ken Coates MEP   75p

Democracy versus Capitalism
A response to Will Hutton with some old questions for New Labour
Michael Barratt Brown with Hugo Radice   £1.50

Feminism after Post-feminism
by Liz Davies   £2.00

May Day
Solidarity, Celebration, Struggle
written and illustrated by John Gorman

The Rights of the Unemployed
A Socialist Approach
by Anne Gray   £1.95

Europe and NATO Expansion
by Frank Blackaby   £1.50

The Yugoslav Tragedy
Lessons for Socialists
by Michael Barratt Brown   £4.99

Common Ownership
Clause IV and the Labour Party
by Ken Coates MEP   £5.99

The Blair Revelation
Deliverance for whom?
by Michael Barratt Brown and Ken Coates MEP
Cloth £35   Paper £6.99

New Labour as Past History
by Royden J. Harrison   £1.50